SMUGGLING LANGUAGE INTO THE TEACHING OF READING

Second Edition

Arthur W. Heilman
Pennsylvania State University

Elizabeth Ann Holmes
University of Oklahoma

The Charles E. Merrill
COMPREHENSIVE READING PROGRAM
Arthur W. Heilman
Consulting Editor

CHARLES E. MERRILL PUBLISHING COMPANY
A Bell & Howell Company
Columbus   Toronto   London   Sydney

Published by
CHARLES E. MERRILL PUBLISHING COMPANY
A Bell & Howell Company
Columbus, Ohio 43216

This book was set in Times Roman.
The production editor was Elizabeth A. Martin.
Cover photo from *Values in the Classroom,* Charles E. Merrill, 1977.
The cover was designed by Salvato Coe Associates.
The cover was prepared by Will Chenoweth.

Library of Congress Catalog Card Number: 77-015683

International Standard Book Number: 0-675-08360-5

1 2 3 4 5 6 7 8 — 84 83 82 81 80 79 78

Printed in the United States of America

Other Titles in Merrill Comprehensive Reading Program

Arthur W. Heilman, *Consulting Editor*

BURRON	*Basic Concepts in Reading Instruction, Second Edition*
EKWALL	*Psychological Factors in Teaching Reading*
MANGRUM	*Developing Competencies in Teaching Reading*
FORGAN	*Teaching Content Area Reading Skills*
GILLILAND	*Practical Guide to Remedial Reading, Second Edition*
HILLERICH	*Reading Fundamentals for Preschool and Primary Children*
MCINTYRE	*Reading Strategies and Enrichment Activities for Grades 4–9*
MAY	*To Help Children Read, Second Edition*
PFLAUM-CONNOR	*The Development of Language and Reading in Young Children, Second Edition*
SHEPHERD	*Comprehensive High School Reading Methods, Second Edition*
STRAIN	*Accountability in Reading Instruction*
WEIMER	*Reading Readiness Inventory*

Preface

Smuggling Language into the Teaching of Reading is an outgrowth of several perceptions about reading instruction. First, many children are not learning to read. Second, many who do learn are turned away from reading because the experiences associated with learning have curtailed their interest in reading. Third, many teachers admit that teaching children to read is often not the exhilarating and rewarding experience it could be.

We can no longer con children into believing that learning to read is a pleasant, rewarding experience if instruction consists of routine, uninspiring tasks. Actually, motivating children to read is extremely difficult unless, while reading, they are exposed to and develop an appreciation for the power and beauty of language.

This book consists of techniques and procedures for teaching reading as a meaning-making, language-oriented process. It starts from the premise that the activities of teaching and learning can be both fun and growth-provoking. This cannot be achieved by devoting years and years to the teaching of mechanical skills and *then* applying these skills in the reading of "great literature." Very early in their reading careers, children must sense that *all* reading is the "manipulation of language."

Before children can cope with chapters and whole books, they must be taught how to "mine" sentences and brief passages of language. They can be taught essential skills while working with these smaller units of reading material. They can be exposed to both the precision and ambiguities of language long before they are exposed to the curriculum of law, medicine, or physics.

While it may be incongruous to talk of smuggling language into reading instruction, the fact remains that children are not learning to read. However, children are fascinated by language, and the school should build on this interest. In the final analysis, language is the only magic available in the schools. We hope this handbook will provide some guidelines to help this magic happen.

A. W. H.
E. A. H.

iv

CONTENTS

Introduction   1

    Language   2
    Language and Reading   3
    The Permanent Substitute Teacher   4

Intonation and Reading   9

    Teaching Intonation Using Color and Number Rhymes   10
    Emphasizing Different Words   11
    Expressing Feelings Through Intonation   12
    Profiting From Punctuation   13

Expanding Word Meanings   15

    Expansion of Meanings   16
    Gradations in Word Meanings   21
    Working With Relationships   23
    Figurative Expressions   27
    Working With Prefixes and Suffixes   33
    Working With Synonyms   36
    Working With Antonyms   39
    Using Homonyms   42
    Synonyms, Antonyms, and Homonyms   46
    Words Often Confused   49

Critical Reading   53

    Analogies   54
    Following Directions   57
    Fun With Words   62
    Detecting Malapropisms   63
    Scrambled Famous Sayings   64
    Finding the Sentence That Doesn't Fit   65
    Drawing Inferences   68
    Thinking While Reading   72
    Sentence Meaning   74
    Stimulating Language—Using Riddles   76
    Context Clues   78
    Interpreting Proverbs   83

Reading, Writing, and Dramatization   87

    Combining Sentences   88
    Expanding Sentences   89
    Gobbledygook   90
    Picture Stories   92
    Building Paragraphs   96
    Writing Descriptions   97
    Oral Language Activities   100
    Dramatization   107

Study Skills   110

    Working With Dictionary Skills   111
    How to "Mine" a Book   116
    Using the Encyclopedia   117
    Using Maps   120
    Developing Flexible Reading Habits   123

Introduction

Our society places a very high value on learning to read. We have staked out a period of time in the lives of our children when learning to read takes precedence over every other goal and activity. Children who do not learn to read cannot lead normal lives in our society. Yet, an observer from another planet might conclude that we teach children to read so that it can be said they have learned how to read.

We would be most reluctant to agree with this analysis, but we do seem a bit hazy as to *why* we are obsessed with teaching every child to read. Some of the more frequently heard reasons are so that children can get through school; learn about the world around them; make something of their lives; interact with the minds of great poets, statesmen, and thinkers; have access to all the ideas, knowledge, and theories that have ever been written.

When all the justifications for teaching reading have been catalogued and summed up, we have a fairly simple statement: We teach children to read so that they have an important tool for developing and expanding concepts.

How to Teach Reading is one question we will probably never stop debating. It is possible to teach reading, criticize reading instruction, or even write a book on how to do it without understanding what really goes on during instruction. It is also possible to discover what does go on in reading instruction and be threatened by this discovery.

We have fallen into the habit of thinking that reading instruction must surely focus on a behavior which we call reading. From this premise it would follow that when teachers are teaching reading they are working with a totality—the reading process. While this may be the way we prefer to think about reading instruction, this is not the way it is.

1

Instruction Focuses on Skills

There are approximately 180 school days per year during which blocks of time have been set aside for reading instruction. Observing the real world of the classroom while reading instruction is taking place reveals that instruction always focuses on one or more short-term goals. Each of these short-term goals deals with children mastering some identifiable skill. If one makes an exhaustive list of reading skills, the list will include what the teacher of any given grade will be doing on the sixteenth, forty-third, or eighty-second day of the school year.

Thus, reading instruction deals with fragments of the total process. However, as these somewhat isolated skills are taught, we keep our eyes hopefully on the ultimate goal of instruction, producing critical readers. Actually, there is a problem here that is much more real than it is apparent. Children cannot read something critically if they lack any essential skill that is required for critical reading. However, since instruction is *skills* oriented, children often perceive reading as being a mechanical process instead of a procedure by which language is used. Like their elders, they confuse reading with the *activities* associated with learning to read.

These skill oriented activities are so numerous that several years of instruction are devoted to them. Teaching and reviewing code-cracking skills can involve so much time and effort that it should be easy to understand why children confuse these activities with reading. The theorist can see that learning letter-sound relationships is in the long run related to critical reading. But, as week after week is devoted to these isolated teachings, children are justified in concluding that this is reading.

The worst possible outcome of this type of instruction is that children fail to see reading as language usage. When this occurs, teachers quite frequently end up asking "How do you motivate children to read?"

Even children who master hundreds of skills, and who in theory could mesh all of these skills in critical reading, have little desire to do so. Their experience with learning to read has not tied reading to language. Instruction did not provide the proper mix of skills and language usage, and when this component has been neglected, children can easily become reading dropouts even after mastering the mechanics of reading.

Language

Observing the social-intellectual development of children during their first six years, one must be amazed at the role of language in this development. Lately, it has been suggested that educators may be underestimating children's grasp of language. It would also be reasonable to suggest that our instructional strategies in teaching reading ignore the tremendous motivational value that resides in language.

While language is a social tool, it is interesting to note children's language usage in situations where no other individuals are involved. In such situations, children use language with a passion. When children are alone, they will play two, three, or more roles, each of which involves language. They soon sense that this highly rewarding behavior is perceived by adults as being a bit odd. Gradually children self-consciously inhibit these double and triple roles when adults invade their life space. They stop talking out loud and begin to conduct their language-play subvocally.

During the late 1960s and early 1970s, there were several television programs in which adults talked to child viewers as if they really existed. Such programs often irritate adults, particularly if they have never really observed how children interact in this language situation.

Language and Reading

The power of language for producing growth is greatly diluted when children enter school. Prior to entering school, their language growth was developed both through hearing models and through use. The latter would qualify as the true measure of language acquisition. The school, possibly without intention, is structured so that a large part of the child's language experience is passive. Much of the time when language is used, the child functions as a *hearer*. This enforced passivity tends to inhibit language growth.

In the schools' defense, it might be reasoned that chaos will result in classrooms of twenty-five pupils if the use of language is not controlled. Perhaps the real issue is whether or not the school's intervention is too abrupt, too thorough, and too rigid. If it is true that spontaneity is stifled, then alternatives to present practices should be found.

All teaching done in the school must pass through the language filter before it becomes learning. There is quite a loss between teaching input and learning outcome. Recently, having discovered pockets of poverty and ghetto children, we also discovered that the language of the school was not a good vehicle for teaching these children. The language of the school was significantly different from the language these children know and use.

The language used in teaching children to read is also quite remote from their experience. Instruction in reading, with its basals, decoding emphasis, study of words, repetition, strange alphabets, color coded cardboard stories, and fat cats on mats seem intent on waiving language in teaching reading. Overdependence on instructional materials which neglect the power of language impairs the effective teaching of reading. Instruction must draw on and extend the rich language background that most children bring to school. Perhaps if we, as teachers, could take the time to reflect on how our teaching affects children, we might wish to modify some of our procedures.

Language is the only magic available to the school; all the rest is routine, ritual, and rote. The magic of language must come through loud and clear in the teaching of reading. If this does not occur, we produce children who may learn the mechanics but whose later behavior gives rise to the question, "How do you motivate children to read?"

One need not resort to a total break with tradition or swear eternal hostility to existing instructional materials. The story of Miss Black, which will be briefly touched upon here, illustrates one option that any teacher can exercise.

As a preface to her story, it can be said that Miss Black had a terrible but beautiful experience. It started with a dream, which was unfortunate. The dream was instrumental in the forming of a national association to save America, euphemistically called DDT (Don't Dream—Teach). This association labeled Miss Black's beautiful experience Black's Bad Dream. However, in the underground Educational Literature, it became known as "The Permanent Substitute Teacher."

The Permanent Substitute Teacher

There are some people who say the whole story is fiction. They maintain there never was a Miss Black, she never borrowed the $20, she never ordered a double scotch and a lobster dinner. The facts are these. Miss Black was a teacher, the first to admit (to herself) that some days teaching was more of a bore than an unmitigated joy. She had experienced several consecutive months of bad vibrations in her classroom. She borrowed $20 from the Amalgamated Teachers' Credit Union and went out on the town.

Whether it was what she ate, drank, or a combination of both, she later that night had a dream (Black's Bad Dream). In this dream she was confronted by a computer and accused of being a party to poor teaching. As often happens in dreams, she reacted irrationally. She immediately pleaded guilty without consultation with the Teachers' Union legal staff. Dreamlike, she thought pleading guilty would be a mitigating circumstance when punishment was meted out. However, it had already been decided that she was to be made an example of, and as punishment she was sentenced to twenty more years of teaching—with the proviso that during this time she was to function as a *permanent substitute teacher!*

Her dream now turned into a nightmare. Monday morning at 7:30, the phone rang, and the computer told Miss Black to report to third grade at Jackson School; Tuesday, it was first grade at Dunbar; Wednesday, sixth grade at Lincoln School; Thursday, back to third grade, but this time at Douglas, and so on for twenty years.

In Miss Black's own handwriting, we are told that she was greatly relieved when she awoke from this bad dream. In fact, she reached a new high because it was Saturday and tomorrow was Sunday. She didn't have to teach at all for forty-eight hours!

Just about this time, the insidious aspect of her experience began to take hold of her. She became convinced that the dream was a harbinger. She had been warned in a dream and what had happened in the dream would be fulfilled in real life.

Without knowing why, she suddenly thought of the story of Br'er Rabbit who was destined to receive the worst punishment Ole Bear could think of. "Throw him in the briar patch," said Ole Bear. "You are a permanent substitute teacher," echoed Old Computer. Miss Black recalled that Br'er Rabbit thrived on his punishment—he actually *enjoyed* it. She knew in a flash that this was the key. There must be a way to make being a permanent substitute bearable, maybe even pleasant.

She sat down and tried to recall those days—any day—that teaching had been fun. She wanted some models; what had happened on good days? Obviously, she remembered the day she almost got fired for being a good teacher. The social studies lesson hadn't been very meaty. Something about the Southwest with cattle ranches, stockyards, huge herds of cattle, horses, and cowboys. The discussion was over and she knew she needed some filibuster material, so she threw out the question, "What other animals are helpful to people?" The whole thing was just short of dramatic.

Then boom! The one kid she always tried to ignore suggested "Let's name animals that are smaller than an average-size fox." Before she could suggest that he go to the office, the rest of the class was off and naming. They not only named, they challenged, debated, rebutted, refuted, and modified original stances. It was the phrase "average size" that got things rolling. This was just the right chunk of language to come before *fox*. The discussion was still in progress when the social studies period ended. As she recalled the situation, she was about to say "Get out your _____" when someone volunteered "mongoose."

Someone was immediately corrected, "You trying to talk French or something? Who ever heard of a mon—it's *man,* like man goose!" Third girl, second row, chimed in with "You don't go around saying man goose, it's '*drake*.' Miss Black recalled saying, "Oh. I believe that's *gander*." Willie, the history buff, supported Miss Black saying, "Yeh, Drake was an admiral." The new kid from Iowa insisted Drake was "the relays." The questions, What's an admiral? and What's a relay? were forgotten when original boy said "No! It's a mongoose! A mongoose is smaller than an average-size fox and it kills cobras."

The room buzzed. An animal smaller than an average-size fox, and it kills cobras. Miss Black recalled saying "Children, let's get out our _____." She didn't quite finish because she didn't really have the floor. "Let's look it up, Miss Black." "May I use the encyclopedia?" "Is mongoose in the dictionary—how do you spell it?" Miss Black recalled there was a tide running and she swam with it.

Yes, they could research the mongoose, yes, they could go to the library, read trade books, read animal books, borrow encyclopedias, use the dictionary, gather facts, compare notes, write a story.

The class learned that a mongoose is
> two feet long, including the tail,
> sixteen inches long,
> fifteen to eighteen inches long,
> ferret-like,
> weasel-like,
> found in India,
> found in Africa, Asia, and especially India,
> known for a fierce disposition, and
> easy to tame.

In addition, the plural of mongoose is mongooses. There are none in the continental United States because their entry is banned by the government. The mongoose kills cobras, snakes, rats, and as one boy said, Ettkuhs. An Ettkuh is a very hard word to pronounce. It is spelled *etc.* Miss Black had to write this on the board: *Etc.* means "and so forth." Everybody learned Etc.

John, who used the dictionary to look up mongoose, read a little too much and came up with a riddle: "What's the difference between *money bag* and *moneybags?*"

No one knew; most everyone thought one was singular and the other was plural. Jane asked John "What *is* the difference between *money bag* and *moneybags?*" And John read the definition from the dictionary which temporarily interrupted the discussion of the mongoose. For two weeks anyone who had a nickel or more was "moneybags."

Three children missed the bus. Two mystified parents called the school, "What was going on there today?" "No, no complaints, but Jill wants a book about the mongoose. Is that a bird that is almost extinct like the whooping crane?" The principal couldn't find the mongoose in the social studies text or basal reader. He said to Miss Black, "May I see your lesson plans for today? What's this about the mongoose? Is that in our curriculum? Do you think we should be discussing the mongoose when the Russians are catching up to us in space?"

It was nice to reminisce, but here it was Saturday, after the Dream. Miss Black had just two days to prepare for her Monday ordeal.

Just then, Pumpelstiltskin appeared. He said, "You have a problem. I will show you how to spin gold from straw." She missed the whole point of his proposal as she replied "I do not need your help, for I have just discovered for myself how to spin gold from straw. I must cease to be obsessed with straw and chaff and let the children spin their soft golden strands of language. Some make golden webs and some, golden sails for "frigates that bear them lands away." Pumpy said "You are mixing your metaphors," and she replied "Yes, golden metaphors, similies, ironies, platitudes, and even ettkuhs."

Yes, it was Saturday, and Miss Black had two days in which to prepare for Monday, which she felt certain would be her first day as a Permanent Substitute Teacher. She wondered to which grade the computer would assign her. She suspected it would be first or fourth, since she was presently teaching third.

After recalling the incident of the "smaller than an average-size fox" and the mongoose episode, she began to feel that perhaps she could beat the system. She had to find ways to work with children's language, to use the power of language to harness their egos to learning tasks.

Miss Black prepared a number of riddles, some kernel sentences to be expanded, a number of fact-or-opinion sentences, a page of true-false statements that cut across just about everything in the school curriculum, some analogies, and a few proverbs.

Monday morning came. The phone didn't ring. Miss Black reported to her third grade classroom. "What a pity," she thought. "I was so well prepared for first and fourth grade and here I am teaching my own third grade." She thought that after working all weekend she should run what they call in the trade *a pilot study*. She would try using some of the materials she had prepared.

About this time, or a few minutes later, she made a startling discovery. Although she had designed language-reading exercises for other grade levels, it was a simple matter to adapt these materials to her present situation. The exhilarating insight stormed through her insight center—that by simply adapting materials, she was ready for any grade level that the computer could assign. In addition, she could cope with individual differences found in any classroom.

She had planned to read the riddles to the first graders because they couldn't read them. However, the third graders could read them, so she put her sheet of riddles on the overhead projector. In grade one she had expected to tease out only six or eight different meanings for the word *set* (set of dishes, set the table, television set, set your hair, a sunset, a set of numbers, etc). Third graders gave fifteen uses.

Several of the fact-or-opinion statements served as the basis for considerable discussion. One which read "Within ten years the U.S. will have a woman president," triggered a number of comments, mostly from girls:

"Women are smarter than men."
"If George Washington was the father of our country, who was the mother?"
"There are more women voters than men."
"If a woman were president . . . "

Someone (average-size fox again) pointed out that all of these things didn't fit in the game. Miss Black switched to working with analogies.

Miss Black reached in her purse for a cleansing tissue and pulled out the clipping. Reading the newspaper a few days before the night of the dream, she had run across something on the sports page that puzzled her. It told of one of the Knicks being closely guarded and eschewing his usual net swishing set shot, used the boards and banked in a tie-breaking two pointer. She had cut this out of the paper intending to have the junior high coach explain it to her—hopefully, as he bought her a cup of coffee.

She changed her plans, read this cryptograph to the class, and asked for a translation. A couple of round ball buffs dug the jive and laid it out for her and the rest of the class. They enjoyed the lucid and illustrated explanations of a bank shot. Someone left his seat and dribbled an imaginary basketball close in to the blackboard. His feet left the floor and practically everyone saw the ball hit the board and go through the net, a perfect bank shot.

You could bank on the fact that this wasn't the end of *bank* and all of its inflected forms. Different meanings popped up from all parts of the room, and Miss Black put them on the board as fast as she could write: fell in a snowbank, curves on roads are banked, sat on the river bank, bankers are not the same as basketball players, a bank is a building, I had a bank book, 9:00 A.M. to 3:00 P.M. are banking hours, a blood bank, never bank on the weather. Someone did it again. She came up with "The guide banked the fire for the night."

This called for an explanation. The explanation led to a discussion of the dangers inherent in the use of fire in forests and woodlands, the damage a recent fire had done in the West, how difficult it was to get a place to camp in national parks. Janet reported a conversation with a Ranger. Joe asked "How many National Parks are there?" and then volunteered "There are lots of bats in Corl's Bad Tavern."

Miss Black corrected the misconception and said, "Now here are some things we might do." When the principal stuck his head in the room, he was pleased and proud. They were reading, they were writing, they were learning, they were enjoying. "What have we going today?" he said. "Why," replied Miss Black, "this is our first annual in-depth study of National Parks and how to preserve them as ecological microcosms for future generations." "Fine, excellent, right on!" said the principal. As he walked down the hall, he toyed with the idea of removing the mongoose entry from Miss Black's folder. She had come a long way since the day she didn't follow her lesson plan.

Miss Black's story is told here because it is believed her experience should not have been labeled a Bad Dream. She encouraged children to enjoy language as part of reading instruction, and taught them that they must read sentences critically if they wish to read chapters and books that way. Not all of the material that follows comes from Miss Black's teaching file. Some comes from other experienced teachers and some from young people preparing to teach.

The exercises in *Smuggling Language Into the Teaching of Reading* can be used as they are presented, of course. However, teachers may find that they need to adapt them as necessary to suit the needs of the students in their classes.

Intonation
and
Reading

It is essential that children, while learning to read, come to understand that what they read simply represents speech. In speech we use many intonation variations such as:

1. Emphasis on a particular word in a sentence.
   (*Really* I am. Really *I* am. Really I *am.*)
2. Pauses in the flow of speech (called *junctures* or *terminals*).
   (Indicated in writing by commas, periods, dashes, etc.)
3. Variations in pitch (low, normal, high, etc.). This might be illustrated by a comparison of how one would deliver the following messages.
   A. Look at that big oil truck.
   B. *Look out* for that truck!
   In *A,* the speaker is calling attention to a truck going by.
   In *B,* his companion is about to step into the path of the truck.

Printing or writing cannot convey all of the intonation signals that are used in speech. However, all of the punctuation marks we use do provide clues to intonation or to what is called the "melody of the sentence." For instance, the three different signals at the conclusion of the following sentence do change the melody considerably.

This is your pencil.
This is your pencil?
This is your pencil!

The following exercises focus on the teaching of intonation patterns and the importance of using proper intonation in reading.

Teaching Intonation Using Color and Number Rhymes

PURPOSE: To provide practice in distinguishing *stress* (emphasis) on words in sentences and to develop skill in listening.

PROCEDURE: Explain the task. Children are to listen carefully to each statement. They are to supply (in unison) a color word in the first group of sentences and a number word in the second group that rhymes with the stressed word in each sentence.

1. Purple grass I've never *seen*
   The grass I've seen was mostly _____. (green)
2. One of the things I like to *do*
   Is color the clouds a nice light _____. (blue)
3. Mother said, Come and have a *drink*
   I've made some lemonade that's _____. (pink)
4. The witch had a *sack* upon her *back*
   It wasn't striped—it was solid _____. (black)
5. I knew two boys named *Ted* and *Fred*
   A funny thing—their hair was _____. (red)
6. Robert was a handsome *fellow*
   He wore a shirt that was bright _____. (yellow)
7. I saw a cat the other *day*
   Its eyes were green, its fur was _____. (gray)
8. If you name a color that rhymes with *man*
   You won't say blue—you must say _____. (tan)

---

1. I saw a number on the *door*
   The number that I saw was _____. (four)
2. The snakes I counted in the *den*
   Were more than six, I counted _____. (ten)
3. The number that will rhyme with *line*
   Is not fourteen, it must be _____. (nine)
4. This number rhymes with *late* and *gate*
   There's only one and that is _____. (eight)
5. If I say the color *blue*
   The rhyming number must be _____. (two)
6. Making rhymes is always *fun*
   To make a rhyme I just say _____. (one)
7. To keep this rhyming game *alive*
   We have to say the number _____. (five)
8. Words like *bee* and *tree* and *see*
   Rhyme with good old number _____. (three)
9. If you're good at doing *tricks*
   You'll make a rhyme by saying _____. (six)

Emphasizing Different Words

Changing Melody of Sentences

PURPOSE: To provide practice in noting how placing emphasis on different words affects the melody and meaning of sentences.

PROCEDURE: Prepare a number of sentences. Write them one at a time on the chalkboard. Read the sentence both *to* and *with* the class. Explain that (1) a question (who-what-when-where-etc.) will be asked, and (2) a volunteer will be chosen to read the entire sentence emphasizing the word (or words) that answer the question.

Example: John wants to ride the boat now.

(Q) Who wants to ride in the boat?
(A) *John* wants to ride the boat now.

(Q) What does John want to ride in?
(A) John wants to ride the *boat* now.

(Q) When does John want to ride?
(A) John wants to ride the boat *now.*

Illustrative sentences:

1. The announcer said it rained hard in Chicago this morning.
2. The train left the station on track three.
3. John found a quarter at the playground.
4. The teacher looked at the picture and said, "Good!"
5. There was no game in Chicago because of rain.

VARIATION: Change questions from "who," "what," and "where" to a more general format.

1. Write this sentence on the board.
    The mother robin hopped across the lawn looking for worms.

2. Ask a volunteer to underline the word that shows that the robin
    a. did not fly or run.
    b. was not looking for seeds.
    c. did not hop on the sidewalk.
    d. was not looking for cats.

VARIATION: Illustrate the function of pitch at the end of sentences.

1. John doesn't *know.*
2. John doesn't know *him.*
3. John doesn't know him *well.*

PROCEDURE: Prepare a duplicated sheet which shows the same sentence several times but with different words underlined to suggest different intonation patterns. A volunteer selects a group (A to D) and says, "I will read a sentence from group A (B-C-D)." The class (or volunteer) then gives the number of the sentence read, i.e. A-1; A-2; A-3, etc.

<table>
<tr><td align="center">A</td><td align="center">B</td></tr>
</table>

A	B
1. *This* is not my coat.	1. The chief died *years* ago.
2. This *is not* my coat.	2. The chief *died* years ago.
3. This is not *my* coat.	3. The chief died years *ago.*
4. This is not my *coat.*	4. The *chief* died years ago.

C

1. This machine will *never* run again.
2. *This* machine will never run again.
3. This machine will never run *again.*
4. This *machine* will never run again.

D

1. "He doesn't deserve to be *elected,*" said Fred.
2. "*He* doesn't deserve to be elected," said Fred.
3. "He doesn't *deserve* to be elected," said Fred.
4. "He doesn't deserve to be elected," said *Fred.*

Expressing Feelings Through Intonation

PURPOSE: To provide practice in noting how different moods or attitudes are suggested by different intonation patterns.

1. Write a number of words on the chalkboard, each of which describes a different emotion.

   anger   fright   happiness   surprise   friendliness   sadness

2. Ask a child to read a sentence from the list below, using one of the emotions described in 1.

   a. Put that thing down, Bob.
   b. I want you to listen carefully.
   c. I got this for my birthday.
   d. Which one of you brought the message?
   e. I can't believe it; of course, it's impossible.

3. After the sentence is read a volunteer is called on who names the emotion detected.

Profiting from Punctuation

PURPOSE: To provide practice in noting the role of punctuation marks as they relate to intonation and meaning.

CONCEPTS:

1. How punctuation marks serve as "signals" to indicate *pauses, emphasis,* and *pitch.*
2. How the absence of punctuation may distort meaning in reading.
3. How proper punctuation helps the reader determine meaning.
4. How changes in punctuation influence intonation patterns and meaning.

PROCEDURE:

1. Present introductory material via chalkboard or overhead projector.
2. Use sentences in which the meaning can be altered by changes in punctuation.

Examples:

1. Father said, Carol come and play.
2. "Father," said Carol, "come and play."
3. Father said, "Carol, come and play."
   (Discuss changes in intonation and meaning in sentences 2 and 3.)

1. That little boy said his brother is dirty.
2. That little boy, said his brother, "is dirty."
3. That little boy said, "His brother is dirty."
   (Discuss differences in intonation and meaning in sentences 1, 2, and 3.)

Changing Meaning

TEACHER: "Add punctuation marks to each sentence B to change the meaning of sentence A."

A. This is my sister Ellen the ice skater.
B. This is my sister Ellen the ice skater.

A. The book said the teacher is unimportant.
B. The book said the teacher is unimportant.

A. Your son said his friend is ill.
B. Your son said his friend is ill.

A. Jerry said David is always late.
B. Jerry said David is always late.

A. All the answers he wrote on the board are wrong.
B. All the answers he wrote on the board are wrong.

Adding Punctuation Marks and Capital Letters

TEACHER: The stories below were written without punctuation marks and capital letters. Put in the punctuation marks and capital letters that are needed to make the stories easy to read.

STORY A

After school in the spring my friends and I would often play baseball we would go to the empty lot behind my house when we were finished playing some of my friends would stay for supper we had lots of fun together

STORY B

The boy came home right after school his mother gave him some cookies milk and an apple he ate everything he said thank you and went out to play wasn't he a lucky boy

Mixed-up Punctuation

PURPOSE: To provide practice in noting how punctuation helps the reader.

PROCEDURE:

1. Prepare brief paragraphs which include deliberate errors in punctuation and capitalization. Children are to rewrite the passages so that they make sense.
2. Explain to students that the passage has the punctuation marks and capital letters "mixed up." When these "signals" are wrong, the meaning gets mixed up. Have the children rewrite the paragraph, changing the punctuation and capital letters so that the "signals" help the reader get the meaning.

Rewrite this paragraph:

Billy listened, carefully as the teacher. Explained how punctuation helps. The reader commas periods exclamation marks and question marks? All help a reader get meaning. From the printed page. Billy wondered what would happen. If the printer got the punctuation marks mixed. Up it was hard for him to imagine. What this would do to a story.

_____

_____

_____

_____

_____

_____

_____

_____

Expanding
Word
Meanings

The dual purpose of the school is to help learners develop and expand concepts and develop tools which permit them to do this away from school. The most important growth gradient with which the school deals is the individual's stock of word meanings. The learning goals of each curriculum area are achieved primarily through written or spoken language.

By the time formal reading instruction is encountered, a child has already developed a good command of the mechanics, or syntax, of his or her native language. The major learning problem is how many meanings the child can program into this syntactical structure. The English-speaking child has some 600,000 words to draw from and arrange into meaning-bearing units. Obviously, only a small percentage of this vast total can be used. However, the size of the child's meaning vocabulary will determine to a large degree the things he or she can and cannot do in a language-oriented society.

Expansion of word meanings depends on experience with language. The exercises in this unit attempt to guide the learner in mastering word meanings and also important facts about the language such as:

1. A given word may have many different meanings.
2. Words may be pronounced the same and have different meanings.
3. Different words may have much the same meaning, yet the differences are important.
4. Words may have both a more or less fixed meaning and special meanings (figurative expressions).

It should be remembered that a particular exercise may present material at one level of difficulty, but this same approach can be used at any level.

Expansion of Meanings

Different Meanings for the Same Word

PROCEDURE: Sentence Exercise

1. Select a common word that has many different meanings.
2. Explain that the purpose of the activity is to use this word in sentences and that each sentence should use the word so that it conveys a meaning that is different from any used previously.
3. Have children supply sentences.

Example: Place on the chalkboard the word *set*. Call for sentences which meet above criteria.

Following are some examples of different meanings for the word *set*:

set the table	ready, get *set*, go
the sun *set*	the *set* in a ring
set of dishes	member of the Jet *set*
set the clock	*set* in mathematics
a television *set*	very *set* in one's ways
a *set* of tennis	the bidder went *set*

Further Examples: Common words which have many meanings—*light, fine, air, mine, fence, press, match, ball, cool, handle, free, head, miss, fly.*

Illustration for Light: one may *light* a fire; turn on a *light*; wait for day*light*; wear a *light*-colored suit or *light*-weight shoes; enjoy a *light* meal; or get caught in a *light* rain.

Illustration for Banked: The old scout *banked* the fire. The storekeeper *banked* the day's receipts. The curves on the new highway were well *banked*. He had *banked* on his friend's help. The player *banked* the ball off the backboard into the basket.

PROCEDURE: Completion Exercise

TEACHER: "Read the sentences below and fill in each blank with one of the words *can, air,* or *fence* to make the sentences correct."

1. "Don't _____ me in," sang the cowboy.
2. Johnny went to the store for a _____ of peaches.
3. Father put the rug on the porch to _____.
4. Our yard is enclosed with a six foot _____.
5. Mother will _____ the fruit for next winter.

TEACHER: "Fill the blanks with the appropriate word, *mine, blue,* or *horse.*"

1. My father worked in the coal _____.
2. I can ride a _____.
3. The dress was _____.
4. "This book is not _____," said Jim.
5. Mary said she felt _____.
6. "When you work, don't _____ around," said Father.

_____

TEACHER: "Read the sentences below and write in your own words a meaning that fits the underlined word."

1. The secretary read the report from the last meeting.

_____

2. We heard a loud report as the motorcycle passed.

_____

3. The spider crawled under the board.

_____

4. The school board held an election last week.

_____

5. The third graders were adding three column problems.

_____

6. A large cement column held up the front porch roof.

_____

PROCEDURE: Matching Exercise

TEACHER: "Read the sentences in column A. In the blank before the word in column B, write the number of the sentence whose underlined word has the same meaning as the word in column B."

A	B
1. Mary was feeling blue.	____a. Discussion
2. The sky was a bright blue.	____b. Curtain
3. The Girl Scouts presented a panel on "Safety."	____c. Unhappy
4. At the window he hung a red and white panel.	____d. Preserve
5. He opened a can of peaches.	____e. Color
6. The lady will can the fruit.	____f. Container

PROCEDURE: Writing Exercise

Use each word below in as many sentences as you can. In each sentence the word must have a different meaning.

can   ball   blue   match   free   horse

PROCEDURE: A Little Heavy on *Light*

Each of the sentences below contains the same underlined word. This word (*light*) has a different meaning in each sentence. Select a definition from the box which conveys the meaning of the word in each sentence. Place the number of that definition on the line following the sentence.

Note: Two definitions in each box are not used.

Definitions (Sentences 1–7)

1. graceful, humble   2. dizzy, giddy   3. to ignite   4. a light year

5. make clear   6. light up the sky   7. a small turnout

8. to treat as unimportant   9. producing smaller products

---

1. The experts predicted a light vote in the election. _____
2. For a heavyweight, he was very light on his feet. _____
3. This new evidence will shed light on the subject. _____
4. The guide said, "Now we will light the fire." _____
5. The area was zoned for light industry. _____
6. Several critics made light of the new play. _____
7. Halfway up the mountain, John felt light headed. _____

Definitions (Sentences 8–14)

1. lighter than air   2. very little quantity   3. understand the situation

4. happy   5. approaching a solution   6. light up the sky

7. little weight   8. clever thief, pickpocket   9. not loud or prolonged

---

8. The prediction called for a light rain. _____
9. I think now we can see the light at the end of the tunnel. _____
10. Winter clothes can be made of very light materials. _____
11. When the speaker finished she received light applause. _____
12. The group around the campfire was very light hearted. _____
13. At last! I'm beginning to see the light. _____
14. Light-fingered Mary received a two year sentence. _____

PROCEDURE: Each sentence on the page contains a blank space. Write one of the words from the clue box in each blank space to complete the sentence.

Clues:	score	handle	cover

1. He's a wise old bird who always knows the _____.
2. The sticker on the carton read "_____ with care."
3. The word _____ indicates twenty.
4. A rug is often called a floor _____.
5. The spy was told, "Always _____ your tracks."
6. She got a splinter in her hand from the rake _____.
7. To get revenge means 'to settle an old _____.'
8. The announcer said, "Oops, Smith lost the _____ on that one."
9. The clerk said, "I'm sorry, we no longer _____ that product."
10. Don't buy the car if it doesn't _____ well.
11. If one team has three runs and the other has two runs we say, "The _____ is three to two."
12. Abraham Lincoln said, "Four _____ and seven years ago . . . "
13. The tall grass provided _____ for the guard.
14. Will the insurance policy _____ the loss?
15. Sixty-five points on this test is a perfect _____.
16. The ambassador said, "_____ this matter with tact."
17. Even though you're angry, don't fly off the _____.
18. Joyce kept _____ for the softball game.
19. The nightclub's ad stated "no _____ charge."
20. The editor told the reporter, "_____ the fire on Twelfth Street."

PROCEDURE: Read the word in the box. Write a sentence on each line that includes this word. Be sure the word has a different meaning in each sentence!

1. run _____
   _____
   _____
   _____
   _____

2. green _____
   _____
   _____
   _____
   _____
   _____

3. charge _____
   _____
   _____
   _____
   _____

4. order _____
   _____
   _____
   _____
   _____

5. mine _____
   _____
   _____
   _____
   _____

6. save _____
   _____
   _____
   _____
   _____

7. fly _____
   _____
   _____
   _____

8. air _____
   _____
   _____
   _____
   _____

Gradations in Word Meanings

There are many words that represent different amounts or degrees of things, attitudes, or characteristics. What words might be used to indicate varying degrees of wealth from very poor to very rich?

destitute   penniless   poor   prosperous

wealthy   billionaire   rich

There are hundreds of gradients in meaning such as *tiny* to *gigantic, frigid* to *boiling, dull* to *genius*.

PROCEDURE: Read the directions for each of the items 1–6. On line B, rearrange the words on line A so that they fit the directions given.

1. *Directions:*   Most frequent to least frequent
   A. occasionally   seldom   never   frequent   rarely
   B. _____ _____ _____ _____ _____

2. *Directions*:   Very skinny to very fat
   A. obese   emaciated   plump   slender   fat
   B. _____ _____ _____ _____ _____

3. *Directions*:   Very cold to very hot
   A. cool   hot   boiling   tepid   frigid
   B. _____ _____ _____ _____ _____

4. *Directions*:   Very small to very large
   A. huge   small   large   tiny   enormous
   B. _____ _____ _____ _____ _____

5. *Directions*:   Very sad to very happy
   A. pleased   sorrowful   happy   miserable   depressed
   B. _____ _____ _____ _____ _____

6. *Directions*:   Very slow to very fast
   A. leisurely   quick   slow   swift   sluggish
   B. _____ _____ _____ _____ _____

PROCEDURE: On each numbered line below, write three words that will fit between the two words listed. If you need help, the cluebox contains words you might use—and some that do not fit.

Clue Box for 1, 2, 3

timid	close	daring	modest	cheerful	adjoining
bored	sad	cheerless	distant	comic	anxious

1. afraid   _____   _____   _____   fearless
2. near   _____   _____   _____   remote
3. joyful   _____   _____   _____   depressed

Clue Box for 4, 5, 6

puzzling	like	flustered	tranquil	composed	
excellent	adore	bad	good	easy	hate

4. love   _____   _____   _____   despise
5. inferior   _____   _____   _____   superior
6. calm   _____   _____   _____   excited

VARIATION: Write a number of words which represent different degrees of

A.   humility
     to
     arrogance   _____   _____   _____   _____

B.   truth
     to
     falsehood   _____   _____   _____   _____

C.   light
     to
     dark   _____   _____   _____   _____

Working With Relationships

Children need practice in seeing relationships and in recognizing characteristics which are essential in classification activities. The following materials illustrate a few formats for developing these skills.

PROCEDURE: Each word in column **A** can be associated with one word in column **B**. Draw lines connecting appropriate words in **A** to those in **B**.

A	B	A	B
coffee	words	clock	direction
trip	snow	watt	time
milk	cup	compass	weight
spelling	map	gram	temperature
sled	cow	thermometer	electricity

A	B	A	B
cat	worm	tadpole	deer
food	ride	cub	cow
robin	eat	calf	lion
bicycle	kitten	fawn	bear
mosquito	insect	cub	frog

Classifying

PROCEDURE: On each line below, three of the four words fit into a particular grouping (games, foods, clothing, etc.). On the line following each group of words, write the word that does not belong in the series.

1. fish, frog, seal, bird _____
2. copper, lead, pottery, tin _____
3. cornflakes, carrots, potatoes, beans _____
4. hat, wagon, coat, shoes _____
5. pencil, chalkboard, paper, notebook _____
6. center, tackle, shortstop, guard _____
7. spade, hoe, rake, hammer _____
8. New Mexico, Mexico, New Jersey, Ohio _____
9. know, knight, knee, kite _____
10. summer, cold, hot, warm _____

PROCEDURE: Read each pair of stimulus words below. On line A, tell how the two are *alike*. On line D, tell how the two are *different*.

Example: chicken—snake

    A Both are alive.
    D One is a fowl, one a reptile

1. snow—river
    A _____
    D _____

2. salmon—goose
    A _____
    D _____

3. shoe—hat
    A _____
    D _____

4. newspaper—billboard
    A _____
    D _____

5. calendar—map
    A _____
    D _____

6. house—barn
    A _____
    D _____

7. love—hate
    A _____
    D _____

8. triangle—circle
    A _____
    D _____

9. dictionary—encyclopedia
    A _____
    D _____

10. brick—nail
    A _____
    D _____

Cause and Effect Words

PURPOSE: . To provide practice in recognizing cause and effect relationships.

PROCEDURE: Think of each word under **A** as the cause of something. Then circle the one response under **B** that represents a logical result of **A.**

		A		**B**	

Example - deluge: sponges   (flood)   canal

1.	research:	friendship	earthquake	inoculation
2.	ignite:	fire	inflation	misunderstanding
3.	precipitation:	float	humidity	umbrella
4.	garbage:	restaurants	concealment	land fill
5.	overkill:	extinction	treaty	uncertainty
6.	arbitration:	union	settlement	chaos
7.	drought:	rainfall	employment	desert
8.	friction:	wear	shock	blight
9.	practice:	fatigue	mastery	discovery
10.	cloudburst:	consequences	migration	flood

PROCEDURE: Read each word in the list below. On the line provided, write a possible result of each word.

Clue Box

harmony   dustbowl   glaciers   deficit   sanitation   laws
erosion   voting   default   meteorite   earthquake   misunderstanding

1. congress_____
2. nonpayment _____
3. overspend _____
4. rapport _____
5. fault _____

6. ambiguity _____
7. drought _____
8. flood_____
9. sufferage _____
10. ice age _____

PROCEDURE: Under each heading below write a list of words that describe that heading. All of the words in the clue box can be used. You may need to use a dictionary for some words.

Clue Box for Set I

nonchalant	smug	proud	calm	arrogant	casual
overbearing	unruffled	poised	jaunty	haughty	composed
assured	overconfident	indifferent	self-satisfied		

Set I

"This cat is cool" words   "Somebody has the big head" words

1.   1.
2.   2.
3.   3.
4.   4.
5.   5.
6.   6.
7.   7.

Clue Box for Set II

calm	skeptical	dubious	affable	suspicious
doubtful	relaxed	distrustful	tranquil	unconvinced
unobtrusive	peaceful	undecided	questionable	serene

Set II

"He's the quiet type" words   "I have my doubts" words

1.   1.
2.   2.
3.   3.
4.   4.
5.   5.
6.   6.
7.   7.

Figurative Expressions

The English language is rich with figurative expressions and idiomatic phrases. These occur with high frequency even in the materials prepared for use in the elementary grades. Since children are likely to think in terms of literal meanings, they need practice in reading such expressions, discussing their meanings, and in using them in their own speech and writing.

Recognizing Expressions

PROCEDURE: Have children underline the sentence in each group that contains a figurative expression. Then, in group work, identify the expressions, discuss their meanings, and devise other ways of saying them.

1. Mary went to the store.
   Mary saw a puppy.
   Mary's eyes sparkled with delight when she saw the puppy.

2. The airplane soared into the wild blue yonder.
   The airplane flew very high in the sky.
   The airplane flew over the city.

3. The boy is a good swimmer.
   He jumped off the diving board and sailed gracefully into the pool.
   He swims every day in the summer.

4. My mother has a new car.
   My mother drives her car to work.
   My mother took off like a bullet as she left for work.

5. We had a test in class today.
   We had to put on our thinking caps to pass the test.
   We had lots of questions on the test.

6. The weather was very cold.
   Snowflakes danced and swirled across the yard.
   Everyone remained in the house.

7. Everyone was angry with Tim.
   Many tried to keep him from succeeding.
   Tim counted every knock as a stepping-stone to success.

8. The old horse nibbled the short grass.
   The old horse was on its last legs.
   The horse was old and feeble.

9. "You're too big for your britches", said his mother.
   "Your pants are too large", said his mother.
   His mother said, "I don't think your pants fit you."

PROCEDURE: Completion Exercise

TEACHER: "Fill blanks in **A** with the word from **B** that completes the figurative expression."

A

1. Her eyes sparkled like _____.
2. The wind was _____ down the street.
3. Trouble seemed to _____ his footsteps.
4. The pilot completed the first _____ of the journey.
5. The boy was as stubborn as a _____.

B

1. dog	4. howling
2. mule	5. leg
3. roar	6. diamonds

A

1. The captain's voice blasted out with a loud _____.
2. The girl has the temper of a _____.
3. He was as hungry as a _____.
4. Losing her ticket put her in a terrible _____.
5. "His check is as good as _____," said the banker.

B

1. spitfire	4. roar
2. bear	5. fix
3. gold	6. mouse

A

1. Hearing the good news made her as happy as a _____.
2. "We'll be lucky to _____ this storm," said the captain.
3. "A penny for your _____," said mother.
4. When you are angry be careful not to lose your _____.
5. He was so frightened, that he turned as white as a _____.

B

1. weather	4. thoughts
2. head	5. lark
3. sheet	6. tune

PROCEDURE: Write a number of sentences which contain a figurative expression. Underline the expression. Write several statements under the sentence that could describe the underlined expression. Have students identify the statement that explains the meaning of the expression.

1. My sister is as <u>pretty as a picture</u>.

   a. My sister is always very still.
   b. My sister is very pretty.
   c. My sister looks like her picture.

2. The pioneers <u>pushed over the mountains</u> to settle the West.

   a. The pioneers knocked down the mountains to settle the West.
   b. The pioneers pushed the mountains over with their strength.
   c. The pioneers crossed the mountains to settle the West.

3. Pittsburgh is <u>the gateway</u> to the Midwest.

   a. There is a large gate through which people pass to the Midwest.
   b. People frequently pass through Pittsburgh going to the Midwest.
   c. Pittsburgh has a large gateway.

4. Her parents were <u>beside themselves</u> with worry.

   a. Her parents were very worried.
   b. Her parents stood beside each other and worried.
   c. Worry was always beside her parents.

5. As soon as school is out the pupils <u>make tracks</u> for home.

   a. Pupils go home as soon as school is out.
   b. Pupils draw footprints as soon as school is out.
   c. Pupils go by the railroad tracks as soon as school is out.

In the fall of the year the forest <u>is painted</u> with many colors.

   a. Many people paint the forest in the fall.
   b. Leaves on the trees have many colors in the fall.
   c. Fairies paint the forest in the fall.

7. Mary couldn't <u>make heads or tails</u> of the map.

   a. Mary couldn't understand the map.
   b. Mary tried to draw heads and tails on the map.
   c. Mary couldn't find pictures of heads or tails on the map.

8. The stock car racer <u>took off like a bullet</u>.

   a. The racer took off with a loud noise.
   b. The racer took off very fast.
   c. The racer took off in a straight line.

Key: 1—b, 2—c, 3—b, 4—a, 5—a, 6—b, 7—a, 8—b

Interpreting Common Expressions

PROCEDURE: Write sentences which contain a common figurative expression. Have students explain in their own words what these expressions mean.

PRESENTATION: Material may be presented by using the chalkboard, overhead projector, or worksheets.

TEACHER: "Read each sentence. Then write in your own words what the underlined words mean."

Example: There is an old saying, "any port in a storm."
In an emergency you have to make do with what you have—something like "beggars can't be choosers."

1. Grandfather said, "Take your time, Tim, take your time."
   _____

2. After the accident Carl mended his ways.
   _____

3. The police are hot on the trail of the bandits.
   _____

4. John was mad but he managed to hold his tongue.
   _____

5. "I don't dig that jive," said Al.
   _____

6. Sharon lost her head and threw the ball to the wrong base.
   _____

7. "What a game," said Lynn. "That was a close shave."
   _____

8. Asked about the quarterback, the coach said, "He's fit as a fiddle."
   _____

9. "Jane nearly bit my head off," said Alice.
   _____

10. The field was alive with grasshoppers.
    _____

PROCEDURE: Place the number of the expression under **A** in front of its definition under **B**. Note: One definition in each set will not be used.

A	SET I	**B**

1. "completely in the dark"   ____ never forgets
2. "has the memory of an elephant"   ____ listening carefully
3. "jumped out of his skin"   ____ found a home
4. "I'm all ears"   ____ doesn't know about it
5. "shake hands on it"   ____ very frightened
      ____ a binding agreement

SET II

6. "turned over a new leaf"   ____ explain the matter
7. "down in the dumps"   ____ to act recklessly
8. "hold your tongue"   ____ change one's behavior
9. "passing the buck"   ____ not very happy
10. "shed some light on it"   ____ blame someone else
      ____ remain silent

PROCEDURE: Find an expression in the box that has much the same meaning as one of the numbered statements. Write this matching expression on the line provided.

Clue Box

"flew off the handle"   "right on"   "mum's the word"

"can't make heads or tails of it"   "he's on his last legs"

"a fine kettle of fish"   "a chip off the old block"

1. "a stiff upper lip" _____
2. "blew his top" _____
3. "this is a real mess" _____
4. "keep it under your hat" _____
5. "like father, like son" _____
6. "at the end of his rope" _____
7. "this is over my head" _____

PROCEDURE: A great number of figurative expressions have been coined which involve parts of the body. Some of these are used to describe a person's appearance:
barrel-chested, weasel-eyed, pot-bellied, moose-jawed, bull-necked, bandy-legged.
Some expressions use the names of parts of the body to express ideas, or to describe
other things.

A. Under each sentence below, write the meaning of the underlined expression.
    1. He was the President's strong right arm. _____

    _____

    2. She was the brains of the outfit._____

    _____

    3. Yes, I know him, he's all thumbs! _____

    _____

    4. The ship sailed into the teeth of the storm. _____

    _____

    5. The chairman said, "Let's get to the heart of the matter. _____

    _____

B. On each line below, write a part of the body that completes the expression.

    Clues: mouth, foot, shoulder, head, face, eye, knee, nose, leg.

    the _____ of a hurricane   gave him the cold _____
    _____ action springs   the _____ of an airplane
    the _____ of the river   the _____ of the stairs
    the _____ of a clock   the _____ of the mountain
    the last _____ of a journey

C. The "eyes" have it.
    There are many figurative expressions which involve eyes. Can you interpret
    the following? "the prophet cast his eyes to the heavens," "in his mind's eye,"
    "that's an eye opener," "old eagle eye," "caught the waiter's eye," "has eyes
    in the back of her head," "she eyed him up and down" Can you add a few
    more?

Working With Prefixes and Suffixes

PURPOSE: To provide practice in building words by adding affixes.

PROCEDURE: Duplicate sheets of exercises and let pupils fill in the blanks with a prefix or suffix to form a word that fits the definition. (The following exercises have the affixes listed. These should be left off the pupils' exercise sheets.)

to bring into a country	_____port	(im)
to carry	_____port	(trans)
a gate or door	port_____	(al)
sell in another country	_____port	(ex)
bus, train, plane, or car	_____port_____	(trans) (ation)

to not trust	_____trust	(dis)
relying upon	trust_____	(ing)
worthy of trust	trust_____	(worthy)

to no longer continue	_____continue	(dis)
without interruption	continue_____	(ous)
not connected, broken	_____continue_____	(non) (ous)
to work with	_____operate	(co)
a surgical procedure	operate_____	(tion)
not working	_____operate_____	(in) (tive)
after surgery	_____operate_____	(post) (tive)

to take out and replant	_____plant	(trans)
large southern estate	plant_____	(ation)
placed well within	_____plant	(im)
one who sows seeds	plant_____	(er)
placing seeds in the ground	plant_____	(ing)

to look forward to	_____spect	(ex)
to feel or show honor or esteem for	_____spect	(re)
to look into, examine	_____spect	(in)
an onlooker	spect_____	(ator)
to meditate or ponder	spect_____	(ulate)

Working With Prefixes and Suffixes (continued)

to play over	_____play	(re)
to show	_____play	(dis)
full of fun	play_____	(ful)
a person who plays	play_____	(er)
it can be played	play_____	(able)

to quit, to stop, to withdraw	_____tire	(re)
exhausted	tire_____	(d)
requiring little rest	tire_____	(less)
annoying	tire_____	(some)

to compel	_____force	(en)
strong, powerful	force_____	(ful)
without force	force_____	(less)
to strengthen or make strong	_____ _____force	(re) (in)

Prefixes: Changing Meanings

PURPOSE: To provide practice in noting the changes in word meanings that are achieved by adding prefixes.

PROCEDURE: Add each of the prefixes in the boxes to the words below the box. Then write the definition of the words that were formed.

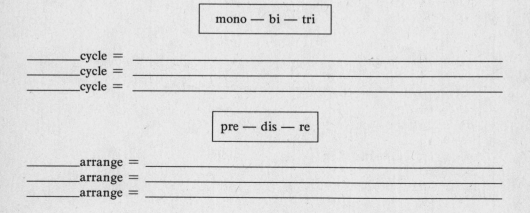

mono — bi — tri

_____cycle = _____
_____cycle = _____
_____cycle = _____

pre — dis — re

_____arrange = _____
_____arrange = _____
_____arrange = _____

Root Words With Affixes

The following material illustrates ways in which students may receive practice in mastery of root words plus affixes.

PROCEDURE: Read each paragraph, noting the meaning of the underlined words.

1. The governor said, "I doubt that the bridge will be built. Doubtless many of you would like to see it built. However, it is quite doubtful that funds will be available." Informed observers agree that this is doubtlessly true.

2. An advertiser spends money on advertising because advertisements help to advertise what he has to sell.

3. A towel will absorb water. This towel is absorbing water. Now it has absorbed about all it can. It absorbs because it is made of absorbent material. The absorption of water is the function of a towel.

4. A just man will never justify injustice. He loves justice too much to attempt the justification of that which is not justifiable.

5. A mountain climber must care about his safety. If one cares he will be careful, not careless. Carelessness in the face of danger does not lead to a carefree climb. When plans are thought out carefully, one is not likely to act carelessly.

PROCEDURE: Write a paragraph in which you use all (or as many as possible) of the words on each line.

1. beauty, beautiful, beautify, beautifully
2. joy, joyful, joyfully, joyous, joyless, joylessly
3. help, helpful, helpfulness, helpless, helplessness
4. war, prewar, postwar, prowar, antiwar, warlike

Working With Synonyms

PURPOSE: To emphasize that different words may have much the same meaning, and to provide practice in working with synonyms.

PROCEDURE: Through group discussion define the term *synonym,* ask for examples, write some of these on chalkboard.

PRESENTATION: Materials may be presented orally, via overhead projector, or as duplicated exercises.

PROCEDURE: Write a word in column **B** that means the same or nearly the same as the word in column **A.**

A	B		A	B
1. right	_____	1. bright	_____
2. above	_____	2. friendly	_____
3. chase	_____	3. cruel	_____
4. dark	_____	4. gay	_____
5. sad	_____	5. leap	_____
6. beautiful	_____	6. awful	_____
7. unpleasant	_____	7. smile	_____
8. clever	_____	8. swift	_____
9. wealthy	_____	9. brave	_____
10. tidy	_____	10. timid	_____

PROCEDURE: The box below contains eight pairs of words with similar meanings. Find each pair of synonyms and write these two words on one of the lines below.

boundary	industrious	comical	dangerous	stretch
weary	allow	brief	border	tired	diligent
expand	funny	perilous	short	permit

1._____   5._____
2._____   6._____
3._____   7._____
4._____   8._____

Synonym Bingo (two or more players)

PROCEDURE:

1. Make several bingo cards with nine, twelve, or twenty-five squares. See illustration.
2. Make lists of pairs of synonyms to equal the number of squares on bingo cards. For example, if there are nine squares on the card, you should have a list of nine pairs of synonyms.
3. Print one word of each pair of synonyms in a square on the card.
4. Decide the rules for playing. For example, the winning card is the first card to have a row of squares covered diagonally, vertically, or horizontally.
5. Read the remaining word from each pair of synonyms to the class.
6. Have students cover the correct synonym on the card with small squares of cardboard, dried beans, etc.

16 squares to a card

9 squares to a card

Right	Beautiful	Bright	Brave	Leap
Above	Unpleasant	Friendly	Swift	Awful
Chase	Clever	Cruel	Tale	Infant
Wealthy	Dark	Gay	Smile	Lead
Sad	Tidy	Astonished	Sick	Tall

25 squares to a card

Crossword Puzzles (Synonyms)

TEACHER: Synonyms are words that have the same or nearly the same meaning. Work the puzzle using synonyms.

¹S	M	³I	L	⁵E		⁷G	L	A	D
W		L		S					
⁹I	L	L		¹²C	O	U	P	¹⁶L	E
F				A				E	
¹⁷T	R	A	M	P			²²L	A	D
				E		²³M	A	D	
¹⁸T	A	L	L		¹⁹L		B		²⁰L
A					O		O		E
L		²¹R	I	V	E	R			A
²⁴E	V	E	N		E				P

Across	Down
1. grin	1. fast
7. happy	3. sick
9. sick	5. flee
12. two	16. guide
17. hobo	18. story
18. high	19. affection
21. stream	20. jump
22. boy	22. work
23. upset	
24. smooth	

Working With Antonyms

PURPOSE: To develop and expand concepts through working with words which have opposite meanings.

PROCEDURE: Explain that the term *antonym* means "words that have opposite meanings." Ask for examples and discuss.

NOTE: After children complete an exercise such as the one that follows, discuss their responses with the whole group. It is likely that there will be differences in responses and noting these differences will also help to expand concepts.

TEACHER: "Fill in the blank with a word that means the opposite of the word in parenthesis below the blank."

1. Bill bought a _____ suit.
   (old)
2. We _____ from the lion.
   (walked)
3. Goldilocks thought father bear's porridge was too _____.
   (cold)
4. The automobile was going very _____.
   (slow)
5. The ball was lost in the _____ weeds.
   (low)
6. They climbed _____ to the top of the mountain.
   (down)
7. The painting was very _____.
   (ugly)
8. The dog had a very _____ tail.
   (long)
9. The fighter was a very _____ person.
   (cowardly)
10. She always has a _____ on her face.
    (frown)
11. The children like to play _____.
    (indoors)
12. The dove is the symbol of _____.
    (war)
13. Cindy _____ the football.
    (found)
14. The pep squad cheered _____ the team.
    (against)

Crossword Puzzles (Antonyms)

TEACHER: "Antonyms are words with opposite meanings. Work the puzzle using antonyms."

¹B	E	³G	I	⁵N			⁶O	
		O		⁷O	P	E	N	
⁸S	L	O	¹¹W					
U		¹²D	E	V	I	L		¹⁵G	¹⁶O
M			T					U
¹⁸M	A	¹⁷N		²¹B	R	I	G	²³H	T
E		O		E				I
R		²²R	I	G	H	²⁴T		S
		T		I		O	
	²⁵T	H	I	N		²⁶P	U	L	L

Across	**Down**
1. end	3. bad
7. close	5. yes
8. fast	6. off
12. angel	8. winter
15. stop	11. dry
18. woman	16. in
21. dim	17. south
22. wrong	21. end
25. fat	23. hers
26. push	24. bottom

Crossword Puzzles—Using Synonyms and Antonyms

TEACHER: "Synonyms are words with the same or nearly the same meaning. Antonyms are words with opposite meanings. Solve the puzzle below using antonyms across and synonyms down."

¹F	A	²S	T		³G	⁴O	O	⁵D
E		N		⁶W	O	N		⁷I	N

¹F	A	²S	T		³G	⁴O	O	⁵D
E		N		⁶W	O	N		⁷I	N
E		O						N	
L		⁸W	R	O	N	⁹G		¹⁰N	O
		S				U		E	
		¹¹T	O	P		N		R	
		O							
	¹²F	R	O	N	T			¹³C	
¹⁴S	U	M			¹⁵F	L	A	T
	R		¹⁶U	P				R	

Across
Write an antonym for:
1. slow
3. bad
6. lost
7. out
8. right
10. yes
11. bottom
12. back
14. difference
15. round
16. down

Down
Write a synonym for:
1. touch
2. blizzard
3. leave
4. upon
5. evening meal
9. rifle
12. animal skin
13. automobile

Using Homonyms

PURPOSE: To expand word meanings.

PROCEDURE:

1. Write a number of sentences, leaving blanks to be filled.
2. Underneath each blank write two or three homonyms.
3. Have pupils read the sentences and write in the correct word to complete the meaning of the sentence.

TEACHER: "Homonyms are words that are pronounced the same but have different spellings and different meanings. Fill the blanks with the correct homonym."

1. We eat _____.
         (meat—meet)
2. I went to the movie to _____ my friend.
                     (meat—meet)
3. The sum of one and one is _____.
                         (to—too—two)
4. We went _____ visit the zoo.
         (to—too—two)
5. His car was _____.
             (blue—blew)
6. Sally _____ out her birthday candles.
       (blue—blew)
7. We walked down the dusty _____.
                     (rode—road)
8. Ann _____ her bicycle to school.
       (rode—road)
9. The _____ was very cold.
     (air—heir)
10. She was _____ to a large fortune.
           (air—heir)
11. At Christmas time we celebrate the _____ of Jesus.
                           (birth—berth)
12. On the train, I like to sleep in the upper _____.
                           (birth—berth)
13. My friend wants to be a _____.
                   (none—nun)
14. The boy would share _____ of his candy.
                 (none—nun)
15. The man worked in the _____ mill.
                     (steel—steal)
16. Thieves _____ what they want.
         (steel—steal)

Concentration: A Game for Pairs or Teams

PURPOSE: To provide practice in working with synonyms, antonyms, homonyms, meanings, of root words, etc.

Directions

1. Select the pairs of words to be used in the game. (Homonyms are used in the illustration.) Write one word on each card.
2. Place all cards face down, shuffle cards, then arrange cards in rows as shown below.
3. Each player turns up two cards hoping to match a pair. If a match is made the player scores two points, and the cards remain face up. If the two cards do not match they are placed face down and play continues. All players carefully observe each play and try to remember the position and identity of each word card exposed. This concentration pays off as the game proceeds.

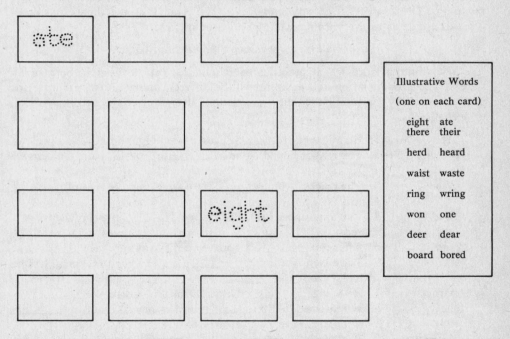

Illustrative Words

(one on each card)

eight	ate
there	their
herd	heard
waist	waste
ring	wring
won	one
deer	dear
board	bored

VARIATIONS: antonyms: innocent—guilty, difficult—easy, generous—selfish

synonyms: huge—enormous, alter—change, ask—inquire

contractions: isn't—is not, won't—will not, I'll—I will

plurals: foot—feet, mouse—mice, goose—geese

Working With Homographs

PURPOSE: To develop the concept that some words are spelled exactly alike but have different pronunciations and meanings.

PROCEDURE: Write a common homograph on the board (wind, read, live, etc.). Discussion will establish that the word has two pronunciations and meanings. Illustrate this with sentences.

"They heard the wind howling through the trees."
"Remember to wind the clock."

Explain that the way in which a word is used in a sentence determines its meaning and pronunciation (at certain instructional levels, it is not necessary to explain the parts-of-speech function, i.e., wīnd—verb; wĭnd—object or noun).

TEACHER: "Some words are spelled alike and yet have different pronunciations and meanings. These words are called *homographs*. The context, or how the word is used, gives us a clue as to the word's meaning and pronunciation.

Many small farms pro duce′ a variety of pro′duce.

The stimulus word which precedes each sentence can be used in both blank spaces. The pronunciation and meaning will be different in each case. Indicate the pronunciation by marking either the vowel sound, līve, lĭve; or the accent, ob′ject, ob ject′."

live	1. He was lucky to _____ after touching the _____ wire.
present	2. The mayor hoped to be _____ to _____ the Citizenship Awards.
object	3. The teacher will not _____ if we bring this type of _____ to class.
close	4. The announcer said, "Thus, we _____ this broadcast of a very _____ game."
read	5. After you _____ a book, you may say you have _____ it.
excuse	6. The coach would not _____ a player from practice unless he had a good _____.
extract	7. He had to _____ the cork from the bottle of _____.
tear	8. When she saw the _____ in her new ski suit, a _____ came to her eye.
contract	9. The _____ stated that the material would not _____ when wet.
address	10. He consented to make the _____ before he obtained the _____ of the meeting place.

VARIATION: Have pupils write sentences which include the stimulus word on the left.

re fuse′ _____

ref′use _____

re cord′ _____

rec′ord _____

lĕad _____

lēad _____

sub′ject _____

sub ject′ _____

VARIATION: Two words are omitted in each sentence below. The words in each sentence are spelled the same. However, these two words are pronounced differently and have different meanings. The first letter of each word is given as a clue. Can you complete the sentence?

1. A r_____ is one who chooses to r_____ against authority.
2. The goal of the p_____ was to p_____ a rocket to the moon.
3. The angry guide said, "I will not d_____ you here in the middle of the d_____."
4. You must e_____ the cork before you can use the e_____.
5. The teacher was c_____ with the c_____ of Billy's written report.
6. Fertile farms can p_____ much p_____.
7. He will l_____ the discussion on the topic of l_____ mining.
8. The king said, "I will not s_____ a loyal s_____ to harsh treatment.
9. The strong w_____ will continue to w_____ the sheet around the clothes line.

Other homographs that might be used in exercises are:

con′duct——con duct′	ad dress′——ad′dress
pur suit′——pur′suit	con′flict——con flict′
prog′ress——pro gress′	mod′er ate——mod er ate′

Find the Wrong Word

TEACHER: "The following sentences may *sound* right, but they should not *look* right to you. Each sentence contains one wrong word. Underline the wrong word. On the line after each sentence, write the word that should have been used."

Example: The opposite of wrong is <u>write</u>. __right__

1. He had to weight more than an hour for his dinner. _____
2. Smokey the Bare is the symbol for fire prevention. _____
3. The teacher asked Jane, "Will you please clothes the window?" _____
4. The movie was about a great heard of elephants. _____
5. Sugar is made from sugar cane and sugar beats. _____
6. Do you know witch came first—the chicken or the egg? _____
7. The whether man predicted showers. _____
8. Have you seen the new golf coarse? _____
9. The Texan said, "I'll take my stake medium rare!" _____
10. The club wanted to raze a thousand dollars. _____

Synonyms, Antonyms and Homonyms

TEACHER: "Stimulus words below are followed by three test words, each of which is a

synonym (S)-same meaning,
antonym (A)-opposite meaning, or
homonym (H)-same pronunciation, different spelling and meaning.

On the space preceding each test word, write the one letter (*S, A, H*) which describes that word's relationship to the stimulus word. One line or series may contain the same category more than once."

Example: right: <u>S</u>-correct   <u>H</u>-write   <u>A</u>-wrong

1. steal	____steel	____take	____give
2. new	____antique	____knew	____recent
3. waste	____squander	____waist	____conserve
4. pale	____wan	____ruddy	____pail
5. scent	____odor	____cent	____sent
6. male	____female	____mail	____masculine
7. soar	____rise	____sore	____plummet
8. coarse	____crude	____refined	____course
9. vain	____vane	____conceit	____vein
10. alter	____altar	____change	____modify
11. cite	____site	____location	____sight
12. weak	____feeble	____week	____strong

Working With Terms Associated With Sports

PURPOSE: To provide practice in

1. reading special terms,
2. associating these terms with a particular sport,
3. writing the meaning for these terms, and
4. creative writing which includes a number of special terms.

Directions: Place several terms on the chalkboard ("no hitter," "goalie," etc.). Call on individuals to identify the sport in which these terms might be used and to explain what the term means.

Directions: Prepare a duplicated exercise similar to those shown below. Have students identify the sport or game with which each of these terms is associated. In the box following each term, write the name of the sport in which the term might be used. On the line provided with each term explain what the term means.

1.   "end zone" ⬚ _____

2.   "triple play" ⬚ _____

3.   "traveling" ⬚ _____

4.   "net ball" ⬚ _____

5.   "fair catch" ⬚ _____

6.   "penalty box" ⬚ _____

7.   "lead off man" ⬚ _____

8.   "fast break" ⬚ _____

9.   "tenth frame" ⬚ _____

10.   "take down" ⬚ _____

PROCEDURE: Read the selection below. Fill the blanks with words from the box that will make the selection meaningful. Use a dictionary if there is any doubt about the meaning of a word.

accept—except	farther—further	advise—advice
quiet—quite	device—devise	whether—weather

The science class was debating w_____ to discuss the local w_____. Some children wanted to do f_____ study and include places that were much f_____ away.

Someone suggested that they d_____ some d_____ for measuring the amount of rainfall. John said, "I a_____ that we seek some a_____ on this matter.

The children were not too q_____ during their planning as they found that they couldn't q_____ decide on all of the details. At the close of the class all e_____ two pupils were willing to a_____ the plans that had been developed.

PROCEDURE: In the space provided, write a sentence in which you use the word at the left.

1. metal: _____
2. medal: _____
3. dairy: _____
4. diary: _____
5. miner: _____
6. minor: _____
7. affect: _____
8. effect: _____
9. cereal: _____
10. serial: _____
11. accept: _____
12. except: _____

Words Often Confused

PURPOSE: To provide practice in working with words that look and sound very much alike and whose meanings are often confused.

TEACHER: "Study the words and definitions in the box. Then, in the sentences below, fill in the blanks with the proper word."

alter:	to change or modify
altar:	place used in worship
medal:	a decoration awarded for service
meddle:	to interfere
cite:	to quote, or use as illustration
sight:	to see, act of seeing
site:	location
council:	a governing group
counsel:	to advise
affect:	to influence
effect:	a result produced by a cause
carton:	a box or container
cartoon:	a drawing, a caricature
miner:	worker in a mine
minor:	young, not of legal age

meddle—medal

1. It might be a good idea to give a _____ to people who never _____ in others' affairs.

alter—altar

2. In over 500 years, no attempt had been made to _____ the _____.

carton—cartoon

3. You will find a humorous _____ on every _____ of breakfast food.

sight—site

4. He hoped to catch _____ of the _____ where the new club was to be built.

counsel—council

5. The city _____ decided to hire an expert to _____ them on this matter.

miner—minor

6. Most states have laws which prohibit a _____ from working as a _____.

affect—effect

7. One _____ of bad weather is its _____ on the price of foods.

Each pair of sentences below contains underlined words that are sometimes confused with each other. No context clue to the meaning of the word is provided.

Directions: Beneath each pair of sentences the words are defined. After each sentence write the number of the definition that fits the underlined word in that sentence.

1. A. One lens in the machine had a convex surface. _____
   B. One lens in the machine has a concave surface. _____
      (1)   curved on the outside   (2)   like inside of hollow ball
2. A. Did the doctor proscribe any medicine? _____
   B. Did the doctor prescribe any medicine? _____
      (1)   suggest as part of treatment   (2)   forbid the use of

3. A. Not everyone uses an alias. _____
   B. Not everyone uses an alibi. _____
      (1)   excuse ("I wasn't there")   (2)   an assumed name

4. A. What is the meaning of elude? _____
   B. What is the meaning of allude? _____
      (1)   an indirect reference to   (2)   avoid, evade

5. A. "I did not imply that," he said. _____
   B. "I did not infer that," he said. _____
      (1)   suggest   (2)   arrive at a conclusion

PROCEDURE: Drill on rapid recognition of similar words

Directions: Read each line of words as rapidly as possible. Practice re-reading the material several times.

1. brand	brave	brake		11. kindle	kindly	kindred
2. duke	dusk	dyke		12. nature	native	natural
3. gnaw	gnarled	gnat		13. wander	warden	warmer
4. emperor	empire	empower		14. glint	glitter	glaze
5. clump	clumsy	cluster		15. detail	detain	detect
6. bundle	bungle	bumper		16. labor	ladle	label
7. amass	amaze	amuse		17. saber	sable	saddle
8. indoors	endorse	induce		18. rubbish	rural	rumble
9. manage	manger	mangle		19. whisper	whistle	whisker
10. glade	gladiator	glamorous		20. knead	know	need

Definitions and Further Clues

Directions: Prepare a separate card for each word concept to be taught. One side of the card should contain the word and its pronunciation. (Column **A**). The other side should contain a definition involving several sentences. (Column **B**)

A	**B**
lob • by ('läb-ē) lob • by • ist (-ē-əst) lob • by • ing (iŋ)	A *lobbyist* is an individual who seeks to influence legislation. He or she may work for the passage of a law or to get a law changed or repealed. *Lobbying* is a legal activity. However, there are laws which govern and control *lobbying* and *lobbyists*.
caste ('kast) caste system	A group of people whose membership in a social class is determined by wealth, birth, occupation, etc. A *caste system* is one in which rules, laws, customs, etc., maintain a rigid class system where social and economic mobility is controlled and discouraged.
mo • nop • o • ly (mə-'näp-(ə) lē)	Control of a product, market or service which permits the seller to control the selling price. *Monopoly* is the absence of competition.
arc • tic ('ärk-tik) ant • arc • tic (ant-'ärk-tik) ant • arc • ti • ca (ant-ärk-ti-ka)	The *arctic* region is the area around the North Pole. *Antarctic* refers to the region near the South Pole. *Antarctica* is a huge ice-covered area surrounding the South Pole.
ap • pren • tice (ə-'prent-əs)	An *apprentice* is one who is learning a trade. In some cases definite rules and conditions must be met in fulfilling an apprenticeship. An apprentice is also called a *novice*. A novice cowboy might be called a *tenderfoot*; a baseball player, a *rookie*.

Directions: Write sentences similar to those below. Have students write their own definitions of the underlined words. If they feel their knowledge of the words is hazy or incomplete, they may add the dictionary definition. Group discussion of items should follow use of the exercise. This helps to clear up misconceptions and helps students use the words.

1. John was in a quandary, as he listened to the report.

    (mine) _____

    (dictionary) _____

2. As she talked, you could tell she was filled with conceit.

    (mine) _____

    (dictionary) _____

3. His interest in reading was dormant for a long time.

    (mine) _____

    (dictionary) _____

4. The family embarked on a perilous journey.

    (mine) _____

    (dictionary) _____

5. The driver had trouble with parallel parking.

    (mine) _____

    (dictionary) _____

6. Her attempt to feign illness was not successful.

    (mine) _____

    (dictionary) _____

Critical
Reading

If one closely examines reading instruction, it becomes obvious that each unit of instruction deals with one or possibly several isolated reading skills. As a rule, we prefer to not think of instruction as being fragmented in this way. We are conditioned to view all instruction, even the teaching of specific skills, in the context of the ultimate goal of instruction—the production of critical readers. This view has some merit since it is true that students cannot read passages critically if they lack any of the skills that are required for this task.

Critical reading is in essence a language manipulating process, and one must translate graphic signs into the language equivalents that the signs represent. To read critically, the reader must have facility with language that at least equals the demands of the material being read.

The school in its everyday operation invariably expects students to deal with larger units of work as illustrated by assignments to read stories, chapters in social science or science texts, or even trade books. This practice is followed even when students have not yet learned to efficiently "mine" smaller units such as sentences and paragraphs. Students who cannot easily determine the meaning of sentences and paragraphs can hardly be expected to cope with chapters and books.

The following exercises focus on smaller units of material for the teaching of critical reading. Students are asked to draw inferences, analyze fact or opinion statements, follow directions, detect malapropisms, and interpret proverbs and famous quotations. The difficulty level varies from first grade (riddles, opposites, etc.) to more difficult levels of interpretation.

Analogies

PURPOSE: To develop critical reading-thinking skills through practice in seeing relationships such as

    1. part to whole ("finger is to hand as toe is to foot"), and
    2. function ("shoe is to foot as glove is to hand").

PRESENTATION: Materials may be presented via chalkboard, overhead projector, or duplicated sheets for individualized work.

TEACHER: "Complete the following analogies by underlining the one word on the right that completes the sense of the statement. Be alert for relationships such as 'part to the whole' and 'function.' "

1. ship is to navy as tank is to	swimmer automobile army
2. bread is to butter as cracker is to	box cheese diet
3. glove is to hand as sock is to	boot shoe foot
4. red is to sweater as blue is to	shirt ocean topaz
5. up is to down as over is to	there under upper
6. bullet is to gun as arrow is to	bow quiver target
7. good is to bad as down is to	under up over
8. robin is to bird as mosquito is to	insect fly net
9. orange is to fruit as carrot is to	stew vegetable food
10. minute is to hour as second is to	first hour minute

TEACHER: "Complete the following analogies by filling in the missing word on the lines provided."

    1. glove : _____ :: shoe : foot
    2. fur : fox :: feathers : _____
    3. tackle : football :: shortstop : _____
    4. _____ : hand :: toe : foot
    5. corn : vegetable :: _____ : fruit
    6. ear : _____ :: eye : seeing
    7. robin : bird :: trout : _____
    8. head : lettuce :: _____ : corn
    9. _____ : sandpaper :: smooth : velvet
    10. collar : shirt :: cuff : _____

Analogies in the Curriculum

English-homonyms: Circle the word that completes the analogy.

1. ate : eight :: beet : vegetable   food   beat
2. wrap : rap :: night : dark   knight   P.M.
3. sent : cent :: nose : knows   face   smell
4. wear : where :: there : place   their   position
5. pail : pale :: herd : buffalo   group   heard

English-plurals: Write the word that completes the analogy.

1. house : houses :: mouse : _____
2. city : cities :: goose : _____
3. girl : girls :: woman : _____
4. tooth : teeth :: calf : _____
5. nickel : nickels :: penny : _____

Arithmetic: Write the word that completes the analogy.

1. 3 : 6 :: radius : _____
2. 3 : 6 :: 4 : _____
3. foot : yard :: one : _____
4. minute : hour :: second : _____
5. gram : weight :: meter : _____

Social Studies: Circle the word that completes the analogy.

1. 3 P.M. : N.Y. :: ____ P.M. : Chicago 1 P.M.   2 P.M.   3 P.M.
2. web : spider :: dam :   beaver   fish   irrigation
3. Canada : U.S. :: U.S. :   England   Mexico   South America
4. purchase : import :: sell :   free trade   migrant   export
5. coffee : bean :: sugar :   sweet   granulated   cane

Science: Circle the word that completes the analogy.

1. plants : botanist :: animals :   geologist   species   zoologist
2. zenith : highest :: nadir :   median   lowest   ghost
3. opaque : transparent :: indigenous :   native   foreign   poor
4. infinite : limitless :: finite :   final   texture   limited
5. extinct : living :: asbestos :   combustible   fibrous   fireproof

Students Develop Analogies

PURPOSE: To provide students with the opportunity for building analogies. This experience permits them to manipulate language as they attempt to express precise relationships.

PROCEDURE: Line **A** lists five words. Use four of these words to make an analogy on line **B**. The words may be used in different order. See example:

Example: **A.** ring   sweater   arm   bracelet   finger
            B. _____ring_____ : _____finger_____ as _____bracelet_____ : _____arm_____
            or _____bracelet_____ : _____arm_____ as _____ring_____ : _____finger_____

1. **A.** tepee   Eskimo   houseboat   Indian   igloo
   B. _____ : _____ as _____ : _____

2. **A.** tall   soft   rock   velvet   hard
   B. _____ : _____ as _____ : _____

3. **A.** fast   short   medium   tall   slow
   B. _____ : _____ as _____ : _____

4. **A.** uncle   parent   niece   aunt   nephew
   B. _____ : _____ as _____ : _____

5. **A.** baseball   sport   touchdown   homerun   football
   B. _____ : _____ as _____ : _____

6. **A.** wolf   man   several   men   wolves
   B. _____ : _____ as _____ : _____

7. **A.** bear   calf   cow   animal   cub
   B. _____ : _____ as _____ : _____

8. **A.** word   language   book   sentence   chapter
   B. _____ : _____ as _____ : _____

9. **A.** stairway   bell   rung   step   up
   B. _____ : _____ as _____ : _____

10. **A.** body   elbow   leg   knee   arm
    B. _____ : _____ as _____ : _____

Following Directions

Reading Directions—1

PURPOSE: To provide practice in critical reading of sentences which provide directions for tasks.

PROCEDURE: Prepare a series of tasks similar to the example provided.

TEACHER: "Read each sentence carefully and follow the directions."

1. Circle all the words to which we could add *ing*.
   car   go   walk   teacher   run
2. Underline all the compound words.
   anyone   desk   pocketbook   park
3. Circle every odd number.
   5   12   24   7   11   18   9
4. Underline every word that rhymes with *man*.
   sun   can   sand   men   fan   ran
5. Rewrite the following words so they make a sentence.
   the   store   lost   the   got   in   child
   _____

6. Make each of the following words plural:
   bird_____   bus_____   spy_____
   dress_____   cow_____   fox_____
7. Circle the words to which we could add the ending *s*.
   ran   fan   can   car   is   this   teacher   girl
8. Underline the words that contain one or more silent letters.
   drum   comb   light   flag   knew
9. Circle each word that rhymes with *me*.
   see   toe   we   face   sea   key   they   sky   she
10. Put the letter *t* in front of each word to make a new word.
    __in   __old   __rain   __able   __all   __end
11. Add the ending *ed* if it will make a word.
    went_____   want_____   do_____
    ask_____   tell_____   call_____

12. Cross out the word that doesn't belong.
    orange   blue   sky   pink   yellow
13. Circle the things that we can eat.
    bread   sand   meat   purple · dress   cooky   brown
14. Write the plural for each word.
    man_____   dog_____
    dress_____   fairy_____
15. Correct all misspelled words in the sentence below.
    we   all   wont   yoo   to   cume   ovir   to   cee   us
    _____
16. Underline the words that rhyme with *cook*.
    stood   book   cork   took   good   book   look   hoop
17. Draw a line under all the numbers that come after *3*.
    7   2   4   1   6   5
18. Put the letter *s* in front of each word to make a new word.
    __and   __hop   __ink   __led   __it   __eat
19. Write the past tense of:
    run_____   sing_____   go_____
20. Underline the opposite of *high*.
    tall   big   low   small
21. Circle the word if it is something you could do.
    hop   house   car   run   boat   read
    one   jump   play   each   sing   work
22. Circle every even number.
    2   9   24   8   31   15   78
23. Write the plural for each word.
    mouse_____   tree_____   dish_____
    dress_____   tooth_____   fox_____
24. List the following letters in alphabetical order.
    b   k   g   c   a   m   l
    __   __   __   __   __   __   __

Reading Directions—2

PURPOSE: To provide practice in critical reading of directions. Each sentence in the exercise relates to the material provided. The exercises are arranged in increasing difficulty. The second exercise deals with concepts left—right, top—bottom, and square—circle.

TEACHER: "Each of the printed directions relates to Clock A or Clock B. Read each sentence carefully and follow the directions given."

1. Put all the numbers around Clock A.
2. Draw two hands to show 3 o'clock on Clock B.
3. Draw two hands to show 7 o'clock on Clock A.

Clock A   **Clock B**

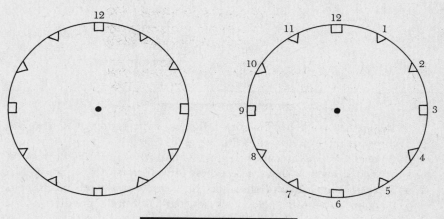

1. Color the circle on the right blue.
2. Put an X in the top square.
3. Color the circle on the left green.
4. Connect the circles with a line.
5. Put a dot in the bottom square.

1. Draw a circle around the two circles.
2. Put an X in each square.
3. Draw a line from S to D.
4. Write a three letter word on line 1.
5. Put a dot in the diamond.
6. Write the opposite of *yes* on line 2.

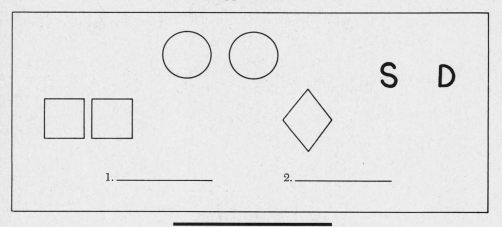

1. If the illustration below contains 5 figures, write *yes* on the dotted line.
2. If there are three circles, put a dot in the first circle.
3. If there are three consecutive figures, each of which is different from the other two, draw lines that connect these three figures.
4. If there are more circles than squares, put an X in the second triangle.
5. If there are as many triangles as circles, put a dot in the middle figure in the box.
6. If the last three figures in the box are triangles, put a dot in the square.

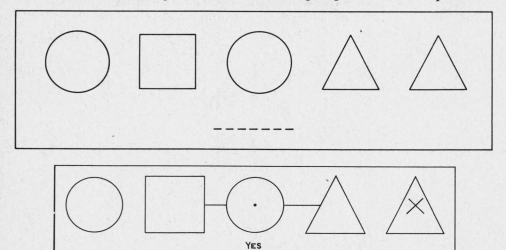

PROCEDURE: Duplicate an exercise page similar to the one shown below. In the illustration the pupils must be able to: (1) read the sentences, (2) know the meanings of *consonants, vowels, square, circle,* and *triangle.*

TEACHER: "How well can you follow written directions? Each sentence below asks you to study the box and then decide if you are to make a mark in the figures beneath the box."

1. If there is just one vowel in the box, put an X in the first circle.
2. If there are more consonants than vowels, put an X in the first square.
3. If the middle letter is a vowel, draw a line through the first triangle.

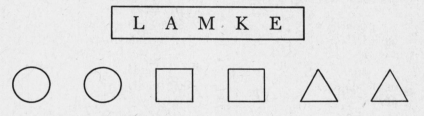

4. If there are two consonants together, connect the two triangles with a line.
5. If there are five different letters in the box, put an X in the second circle.
6. If the letter M follows a consonant, draw a circle in the second square.
7. If the second and third letters spell a word, draw a line under the two squares.

PROCEDURE: Change of Pace

•   •

1. Connect any two dots with a horizontal line.
2. Draw a vertical line which connects two dots.
3. Add a straight line that will complete a triangle.

•   •

Fun With Words

PROCEDURE: Work with expressions similar to the following: What is a disc jockey? a hash slinger? a private eye? A slang term for a psychiatrist is a head shrinker or shrink. Could a psychiatrist also be called a "mind sweeper"? Or "a private ear"? Could a dietician be identified as an "intake engineer"? Or a surgeon as "a real cut up"?

Directions: Number the phrases under **B** so that each one is associated with an occupation under **A**.

A	**B**
1. potter	_____ "has lots of pull"
2. jockey	_____ "earns from urns"
3. receptionist	_____ "oh, my aching back"
4. chiropractor	_____ "just horsing around"
5. dentist	_____ "people greeter"
6. electrician	_____ "a car herder"
7. mathematician	_____ "flour power"
8. baker	_____ "watts my line"
9. truck driver	_____ "boob tube dude"
10. T.V. repairman	_____ "knows all the angles"
11. mechanic	_____ "write on, man"
12. plastic surgeon	_____ "it could be love"
13. author	_____ "lives on lemons"
14. anesthetist	_____ "saves face"
15. tennis player	_____ "sleep merchant"

Detecting Malapropisms

PURPOSE: To teach critical reading, noting words that "do not fit."

PROCEDURE:

1. Explain that people sometimes confuse words. They use one word when they really mean to use another. The words confused are often similar in sound or spelling.
2. Develop a series of sentences each of which contains a malapropism.

TEACHER: "There is one word in each sentence that 'does not fit.' Underline this word. In the blank space following each sentence, write the word you think was intended.

1. May I have the vanilla folder? _____
2. Anna was absent because she had the chicken-pops. _____
3. At the museum we saw the Egyptian mommy. _____
4. The word "big" is a cinnamon for "large." _____
5. Conversation experts fight forest fires. _____
6. She was proud of her long blonde trestles. _____
7. The government banned germ welfare. _____
8. They made many New Year's revolutions. _____
9. John's father couched the baseball team. _____
10. Some people use lemon with tea and some use sugar. I prefer the ladder. _____
11. Children should inspect their parents' wishes. _____
12. That is a very good offer; you should except it. _____
13. Hurry and distinguish the fire before it spreads. _____
14. We watched the cowboys riding bulls at the radio. _____
15. The cantelopes ran across the field. _____
16. The alphabet contains vowels and constants. _____
17. Firefighters get water from a fire hydrogen. _____
18. The land along the river was very futile. _____
19. She chose the lasso of two evils. _____
20. "As you sow, so shall you also weep." _____
21. The garbage scowl chugged up the river. _____
22. In geometry we study squares, angels, and circles. _____
23. Her condition approved at the hospital. _____
24. Riding the alligator is much faster than climbing the steps. _____

Scrambled Famous Sayings

PURPOSE: To provide practice in critical reading.

PROCEDURE: Prepare sheets of scrambled famous sayings. Have students write the sayings in their proper form.

Example:

stitch in a time nine saves.
A stitch in time saves nine.
_____

1. before leap look you.

   _____

2. bush a hand is bird two in the worth in the.

   _____

3. many cooks too spoil the broth.

   _____

4. invention is mother of necessity the.

   _____

5. runs still water deep.

   _____

6. stone gathers no a rolling moss.

   _____

7. makes waste haste.

   _____

8. nature law first self-preservation the is of.

   _____

9. saved penny a is earned penny a.

   _____

10. worm bird catches the early the.

    _____

11. of a flock feather together birds.

    _____

12. one better are two than heads.

    _____

Finding the Sentence That Doesn't Fit

PURPOSE: To provide practice in noting context clues and specifically finding a sentence in a paragraph that "does not fit."

PROCEDURE: Duplicate a page which contains several unrelated paragraphs (samples shown below). Each paragraph will contain a sentence that "does not fit." Have students underline those sentences.

Directions: Read each paragraph carefully and underline the sentence that does not fit, or which does not make sense in the paragraph.

1. Tommy was baking a cake for Mother's birthday. He sifted flour, added two eggs, and put it in the oven to bake. It seemed to take forever to be done. At last the potatoes were ready. The frosting was chocolate with marshmallows.

2. Spot is a little brown and white dog. He is only six months old. A cat has nine lives. Spot loves to run and play. He plays tag with his tail, and hide and seek with us. All day long he runs and plays in the sun. When he gets tired, he just plops down and goes to sleep.

3. I like to play baseball with my friends after school. Sometimes we play on Saturday. We wear white shirts and red baseball caps. Boots and mittens keep us warm. After we finish playing ball, we have Kool-Aid and cookies at my house. I wish we could play baseball every day.

4. Betty went fishing with her father. They left very early in the morning. Betty had made a picnic lunch. It was very good. Mother did the wash. After eating lunch they fell asleep and never did catch any fish.

5. Busy beavers are smart and work hard. They have very large, sharp teeth, and are able to cut down small trees with them. Their webbed hind feet are for swimming. He can blow water out of his trunk. Beavers can build dams in streams.

6. There are many different kinds of animals. Horses and cows live on farms. Farmers raise corn and wheat. Dogs and cats are pets. Wild animals such as lions and tigers are found in the zoo.

7. Three men ran out of the bank and rode away in a cloud of dust. Dust is very fine and gets into everything. The bank had been robbed. The sheriff rounded up a posse and rode after the robbers.

8. Aquariums are fun. You can get fish of many shapes and colors. Frozen fish are handled in many stores. Feeding time is lots of fun. When you sprinkle food on the water the fish swim quickly to get it.

Fact or Opinion Sentences

PURPOSE: To provide practice either in listening or critical reading to determine if sentences are statements of "fact" or of "opinion."

PROCEDURE (ORAL):   Pupils prepare "scratch-paper answer sheet" by writing a column of numbers 1 to 20. Teacher gives the number of a sentence and reads the sentence. Pupils write O (opinion) or F (fact) for each sentence read. Prepare duplicated exercise using sentences such as those shown below.

Group 1

Directions: Read each sentence. If the sentence states a *fact*, write **F** in front of sentence. If the sentence states an *opinion*, write **O.**

_____ 1. We get white milk from brown cows.
_____ 2. Trees grow from seeds.
_____ 3. When you eat a sandwich, you should drink milk with it.
_____ 4. A duck has wings.
_____ 5. All words contain at least one vowel.
_____ 6. George Washington was our greatest president.
_____ 7. Boys are taller than girls.
_____ 8. Sunday is the best day of the week.
_____ 9. A building for farm animals is called a barn.
_____10. The fall season is very much like winter.

Group 2

_____ 1. Within ten years the U.S. will have a woman president.
_____ 2. The Pacific Ocean is the largest ocean in the world.
_____ 3. Large cities are not good places to live.
_____ 4. Eating carrots every day will help you to see better.
_____ 5. February is the shortest month of the year.
_____ 6. We will have astronauts on Mars in the near future.
_____ 7. An opinion may not be a fact.
_____ 8. The earth revolves around the sun.
_____ 9. Americans are the kindest people in the world.
_____10. The month of February may have either twenty-eight or twenty-nine days.

Group 3

_____ 1. Laws should apply equally to every individual.
_____ 2. Freedom of the press is essential for maintaining a free society.
_____ 3. Color blindness is not found among women.
_____ 4. Man will never be able to land on Mars.
_____ 5. The statement "Truth is stranger than fiction" is fiction.
_____ 6. The explosion of atomic bombs has caused changes in the world's weather patterns.
_____ 7. Different brands of aspirin are essentially the same.
_____ 8. Harsh penalties will deter major crimes.
_____ 9. The aim of advertising is to control people's behavior.
_____10. Students should not discuss controversial topics in school.

VARIATION: "After each statement below write **agree** or **disagree.** Then defend your choice in the space provided.

1. Spending money on national defense helps to maintain peace. _____

2. Violence on television is a factor in producing violent behavior. _____

3. Air travel is safer than any other method of transportation. _____

4. Intelligent individuals are usually free of prejudice. _____

5. The very rich do not pay a fair share of taxes. _____

Drawing Inferences

PURPOSE: To provide practice in drawing inferences or conclusions which are not specifically stated in the material.

PROCEDURE: Exercises similar to the following may be duplicated for seat work, or the material may be placed on transparencies for use with an overhead projector.

1. The moving van stopped in front of the empty house.
   (a) The truck was probably empty.
   (b) The truck was there to pick up furniture.
   (c) The truck contained furniture of the people moving into the house.

2. The airplane picked up speed as it came down the runway.
   The airplane . . .
   (a) is landing at the airport.
   (b) is taking off.
   (c) is taxiing to the hangar.

3. The taxicab made a U-turn on Twelfth Street.
   The driver . . .
   (a) saw a man who wanted a cab.
   (b) was practicing U-turns.
   (c) thought a police officer was following him.

4. Coming out of the barbershop, the man put his hand on his head and rushed back into the barbershop.
   The man . . .
   (a) wanted to get a haircut.
   (b) had forgotten to phone his wife.
   (c) had left his hat in the barber shop.

5. All day the wind made a whistling sound through the barren trees. It was probably a day . . .
   (a) in early June.
   (b) in the middle of December.
   (c) near the Fourth of July.

6. Mother looked out the window and said, "There will be no picnic today."
   Mother saw that . . .
   (a) a truck was blocking the driveway.
   (b) the neighbors were going fishing.
   (c) it was raining very hard.

Reading for Inference

PURPOSE: To provide practice in critical reading.

PROCEDURE: Prepare exercises on stencils to be duplicated so that each student can check the correct answer on his or her own paper, or prepare exercises on transparencies for the overhead projector and let students read the exercises and write the correct answers on a separate sheet of paper.

Examples:

She shivered as she walked across the campus toward her class. The sun made patterns on the sidewalk as it defined the leafless trees. "Two more weeks," she thought. "Two more weeks until vacation, and then I'll see Tom." She turned up her collar before climbing the steps and entering the ivy-covered building.

1. What does this girl do?
   a. She works in a factory.
   b. She is a student.
   c. She is a housewife.
2. How old is this girl?
   a. Between 10 and 12.
   b. Between 18 and 21.
   c. Between 35 and 40.
3. Who is Tom?
   a. Her boyfriend.
   b. Her brother.
   c. Her son.
4. What is the weather like?
   a. Cold and overcast.
   b. Cold and sunny.
   c. Warm and sunny.

Fifteen dollars; only five more to go. Soon she will be able to get that cute little ball of fur that wags its tail at her every day. He looks so lonely sitting in the store window. If Jane can get a few more baby sitting jobs, she will be able to show him all the love a ten-year-old has to give.

1. What wagged its tail at Jane?
   a. cat b. dog c. monkey

2. Where did Jane see the "ball of fur"?
   a. her friend's house b. grocery store c. pet store

3. How much money does the pet cost?
   a. $20 b. $5 c. $15

4. Where is Jane getting the money?
   a. her mother b. bank c. earning it

5. How does Jane feel about pets?
   a. dislikes them b. loves them c. never thinks about them

Tomorrow is the big day. John has been practicing ever since school started. Now is his chance to show all his friends his special tricks. This is the time of year when spooky things are really popular. He doesn't even need to wear a costume to scare people. After the parade the older kids get to put on a show for the little ones. Gee! it will be great fun to see their faces turn white. It's a good thing it will be on the last day of the school week. They will have the weekend to recover from their fright.

1. What day of the week will something important take place?
   a. Saturday   b. Sunday   c. Friday

2. How long has John been practicing?
   a. about two weeks   b. about two months   c. about two hours

3. What kinds of tricks will John do at the show?
   a. knife tricks   b. scary tricks   c. rope tricks

4. What holiday do you think it is?
   a. Halloween   b. Christmas   c. Easter

5. What children will see the show?
   a. college students   b. elementary children   c. high school children

---

Edith stared blankly out of the window as Mr. Jones repeated his directions. Edith saw all the rest of her friends begin to fill their papers as quickly as they could move their pencils. If only that late, late show last night hadn't been about the vampires. She certainly could have put her time to better use if she didn't enjoy horror movies so much. Multiplication of fractions was not the topic of the movie, so Edith may have a little trouble completing this morning's assignment.

1. Where was Edith?
   a. home   b. school   c. movie

2. What was she supposed to do?
   a. read a book   b. give a speech   c. take a test

3. Who was Mr. Jones?
   a. a friend   b. a teacher   c. Edith's father

4. What kind of test did Edith have to take?
   a. reading   b. English   c. mathematics

5. When did Edith go to bed the night before?
   a. 2:00 A.M.   b. 8:00 P.M.   c. 10:00 P.M.

Slowly the battered green canoe cut its path through the murky water. Jim lowered his head when he felt trickles of water from the green overhanging branches go down the back of his neck. At the cave's outlet three turtles dived once again into the brown water from their perch upon several rotten logs. After clearing away the debris of sticks and bark, his strokes acquired a steady, even rhythm. Perhaps those canoe races at scout camp last summer were what gave him this confidence. Never had he seen these waters so high or the current so strong.

1. The season of the year suggested is
   a. fall   b. winter   c. summer

2. The weather has been
   a. rainy   b. hot   c. cool

3. Jim is
   a. an older man   b. a young man   c. a middle-aged man

4. Jim was paddling his canoe in
   a. a river   b. a small pool   c. an ocean

The loud and long wail broke the silence of the night. In the sky could be seen the telltale signs of orange streaks. Lights went on in the darkened homes around the block and windows were quickly raised by the sleepy residents. Barking dogs and shivering people soon lined the icy street to watch the long, sleek, red trucks whiz by with their sirens moaning the news. What had been a sleeping neighborhood was now a frantic beehive of commotion and anxiety.

1. What was the danger?
   a. flood   b. fire   c. tornado

2. What were the people watching along the street?
   a. an ambulance   b. police car   c. fire engines

3. What season of the year was it?
   a. spring   b. winter   c. fall

4. Where did the story take place?
   a. a city   b. a farm area   c. a small town

5. What time of day was it?
   a. noon   b. early morning   c. afternoon

Thinking While Reading

In many of the following items one important task is to figure out what the problem involves. The material demonstrates that reading involves thinking even when one is dealing with small units of material.

Directions: Read each of the following items. Then circle the one correct answer from among those provided.

1. To saw a thirty-foot board into six-foot lengths you must saw the board five times. True   False

2. If the radius of one circle is half the length of the diameter of another circle, the circumferences of the circles are the same. True   False

3. There are two brothers, each of whom has a brother. The least number of boys that could possibly be in this family is: four   three   two

4. When the top of a map is north, then west will always be to the left of the map. True   False

5. Every month has at least four Sundays. True   False

6. Circle A has a diameter of four inches. Circle B has a radius of three inches. Circle A can fit inside of circle B. True   False

7. A bottle and a cork together cost $1.05. The bottle costs ninety-five cents more than the cork. How much does the bottle cost? .90   .95 $1.00

8. Opposite sides of a square need not be parallel. True   False

9. If the base of a square is two inches long, the perimeter of the square is six inches   eight inches   ten inches.

10. A nation is more likely to demobilize during a war than after the war is con-concluded. True   False

11. Franklin D. Roosevelt was elected president of the United States four times. True   False

12. One century is equal to twenty decades. True   False

Answer Key: 1. false 2. true 3. two 4. false 5. true 6. true 7. $1.00 8. false 9. eight 10. false 11. true 12. false

VARIATION: Read each statement. Then write the correct answer on the space provided.

1. A is taller than B and C is shorter than B.
   Can A and C be the same height? _____
   Is B the shortest of the three? _____
   Who is the tallest of the three? _____

2. The letters ILIN represent the abbreviations for two adjacent states in the U.S. These states are _____ and _____ .

3. Place the correct number in the blank space.
   a) 1   4   9   16   25   ____
   b) 1   5   10   16   23   ____
   c) 2   4   3   6   5   ____

4. Lemac spelled backwards is _____ .

5. Twin boys aged ten years each have a younger sister. How many children are there in this family? _____ .

6. If it is 9:00 A.M. in Denver, the time in Philadelphia is _____ .

7. The word <u>educated</u> contains _____ syllables.

8. Three girls standing in a straight line each have an equal number of cookies. The girl on the right is the tallest. All of the girls together have two dozen cookies. The girl next to the tallest girl has how many cookies? _____

9. In the blank spaces write the word which does not belong in the series.
   a) dog   cat   rat   snake   rabbit _____
   b) kitten   horse   calf   puppy   cub _____
   c) center   end   tackle   pitcher   guard _____

Key: (1) no, no, A (2) Illinois, Indiana (3) 36, 31, 10 (4) camel (5) three (6) 7:00 A.M. (7) four (8) eight (9) snake, horse, pitcher

Sentence Meaning

PROCEDURE: Sentence meaning exercises consist of statements which students will identify as being either true or false. Each statement contains one or more words whose meaning is being taught or tested.

This type of exercise is not used simply as a true-false test but rather as a means of developing word meanings or concepts. Therefore, papers are never collected and graded by the teacher. They are scored or discussed in a class or group situation. When different answers for an item are found the item is discussed and the use of dictionaries is encouraged in this discussion.

Example:

_____The circumference of a circle is equal to its periphery. (true)

Some students mark the statement false because they think of one meaning of peripheral as "being outside of" or "away from, external." However, periphery is defined as a boundary line and circumference is cited as a synonym

The following materials illustrate series of items for teaching general vocabulary and also terms associated with social studies, arithmetic and science.

Directions: Read each sentence. If the sentence is a true statement, place a **T** in the space before the number. If the sentence is false, write **F.**
General vocabulary
_____ 1. It is illegal to build a replica of a natural monument.

_____ 2. A bibliography is not the story of a person's life.

_____ 3. Siblings must be brothers and sisters.

_____ 4. One cannot paraphrase a court decision.

_____ 5. Homonyms are words pronounced the same but having different spellings and different meanings.

_____ 6. Skeptical means one who is easily fooled or misled.

_____ 7. An alien may become a citizen of the United States.

_____ 8. The term mammoth cave means a very large cave.

_____ 9. An aquaduct is a tropical water bird.

_____10. The term canine includes all breeds of cats.

Concepts from Social Studies

_____ 1. A lagoon is an animal found in the tropics or other warm climate.

_____ 2. An island must be surrounded by water.

_____ 3. Man-made materials are called synthetics.

_____ 4. A serf is one who makes his living off the sea.

_____ 5. A high mountain peak is called a ravine.

____ 6. <u>Sorghum</u> looks like corn and is used as a feed for animals.

____ 7. <u>Irrigation</u> is a method used by farmers to drain flooded farmland or swampy area.

____ 8. An <u>immigrant</u> is a person who leaves his home and settles in a new country.

____ 9. <u>Fallow fields</u> are fields which do not have crops planted in them.

____10. If a nation has a <u>low literacy rate</u>, most of its people can read and write.

Arithmetic

____ 1. A circle cannot be <u>bisected</u>.

____ 2. The radius of a circle is twice the length of its <u>diameter</u>.

____ 3. A square has four sides that are equal and encloses four angles that are equal.

____ 4. A <u>meter</u> is longer than a yard.

____ 5. Twenty decades are equal to one <u>century</u>.

____ 6. A <u>pentagon</u> is a five sided figure.

____ 7. Parallel lines can never <u>intersect</u>.

____ 8. No sides of a <u>trapezoid</u> are parallel.

____ 9. A <u>kilometer</u> is equal to a thousand feet.

____10. If two squares are <u>congruent</u> they are equal.

Science Terms

____ 1. <u>Fossil fuels</u> are formed from the remains of plants and animals.

____ 2. Electrical current flows freely through <u>insulators</u>.

____ 3. Snow and hail are forms of <u>precipitation</u>.

____ 4. A <u>glacier</u> is a huge mass of ice formed on land.

____ 5. <u>Asbestos</u> is a substance that burns easily.

____ 6. <u>Monsoon</u> is a type of monkey widely used in medical experiments.

____ 7. <u>Craters</u> can be formed by meteorites striking the earth.

____ 8. Zoos contain animals that are <u>extinct</u>.

____ 9. A <u>nebula</u> is a large cloud of dust and gas in space.

____10. A <u>decibel</u> is a unit of measurement for the loudness of sounds.

Stimulating Language—Using Riddles

Riddles should be used in reading because they are fun, highly motivating, and can lead to valuable insights about language. Teachers have observed pupils' behavior in their reading of children's newspapers (e.g., *My Weekly Reader*). When children are permitted to select what they wish to read first, they tend to choose the language games such as riddles, puzzles and jokes. We should profit from such observations since children are indicating they enjoy humor and the challenge of sophisticated language usage.*

Riddles provide many different experiences with language. There are language surprises, plays on words, and sudden twists in meaning. Riddles provide a contrast to and escape from textbook language and from the fact-oriented curriculum. Working with riddles helps to develop language facility and the ability to manipulate language.

PROCEDURE: Present riddles orally while the children volunteer answers. If children have the required skills, the material may be printed. Written answers may then be compared.

1. What goes up a hill without moving? (a road)
2. How are a cornfield and an elephant alike? (they both have ears)
3. How can you fix a loose tooth? (with toothpaste)
4. What goes down a hill without moving? (a fence)
5. How do you raise eggs in a garden? (grow eggplants)
6. Which are the best letters to eat? (those in alphabet soup)
7. What has a foot at each end and one in the middle? (a yardstick)
8. How is an elephant like a tree? (both have a trunk)
9. Name one dog that doesn't bark. (a hotdog)
10. What has eyes but can't see? (a potato)

Riddles Based on Spelling of Words

1. What is round at both ends and high in the middle? (Ohio)
2. Which river sees better than any other river? (the Mississippi—it has four i's)
3. What part of a house needs a doctor? (the windows: they always have a pane)
4. What is the only word you can make longer? (long)
5. How can you change a pin into a tree? (add an *e* to the pin)
6. What vowels have three letters? (u—you; i—eye; a—aye)
7. What word can you make shorter by making it longer? (short)
8. How can you change a bee into a vegetable? (add the letter *t*—beet)

---

*Arthur W. Heilman, *Principles and Practices of Teaching Reading,* 4th Edition, Columbus, Ohio: Charles E. Merrill Publishing Company, 1977. P. 161.

Play on Words. Can You Solve the Following Riddles?

If you need help use the clue box.

1. Name one key that is hard to turn.
2. If a chicken could talk, what language would it use?
3. What's worse than raining cats and dogs?
4. When is it not possible for astronauts to land on the moon?
5. Why is it so expensive to feed birds in the winter?
6. What was the box turtle doing on the turnpike?
7. Why did the teacher wear dark glasses?
8. When are truck drivers not people?
9. What is as smart as a horse that can count?
10. Why did the bald headed man throw his keys away?

Clue Box

Answers: (1) a don key (2) fowl language (3) hailing taxicabs (4) when it's full (5) they eat a peck at a time (6) about one mile an hour (7) because his class was so bright (8) when they turn into a rest stop (9) a spelling bee (10) he had already lost his locks

Wild Ones!

If you have trouble with any item, answers are found in the clue box. The answers are not in the same order as the riddles.

1. When is a door not a door?
2. What has fourteen feet and sings?
3. Name two things one doesn't eat for dinner.
4. What's the difference between a tuna fish and a piano?
5. Why is the Pacific Ocean so restless?
6. April showers bring May flowers, but what do May flowers bring?
7. How can you tip over a full glass without spilling any water?
8. Why is an elephant a poor dancer?
9. Why did Freud take hay to bed?
10. What prevents an anteater from having a nose twelve inches long?

Clue Box

fill it with sand; it wouldn't be a nose, it would be a foot; to feed his nightmares; a quartet plus a trio; Pilgrims; it has rocks in its bed; breakfast and lunch; when it's ajar; it has two left feet; you can tune a piano, but you can't play a tuna

Context Clues

PURPOSE: To provide children with experiences which focus on using context clues while they read. Exercises which follow emphasize that context clues are useful for solving unknown words and for arriving at the intended meaning. The missing word (or *cloze*) technique is used in several different formats.

Directions: Complete each sentence by filling the blank space with a word that is found in the sentence. (This time that word will have a different meaning).

   1. Will you be able to train the monkey to ride on the toy _____?
   2. The principal gave a _____ on the new report cards.
   3. The space capsule had very little _____ for the crew.
   4. Some radio stations invite listeners to _____ their views on the air.
   5. The committee planning the _____ said, "Let's hope for a fair day!"
   6. The troops were unable to build a fire because they were under _____.
   7. The music instructor said, "Please _____ how long I hold this note."
   8. _____ this be the reason he yelled with all his might?
   9. The slogan read, "Check cancer with a _____."
  10. "That bowling alley is a gold mine, and I wish it were _____," he added.

PROCEDURE: Associating Paired Words

PURPOSE: To provide practice in using context clues.

Directions: Explain the concept of word pairs, "If I say bread, you would say _____." (butter) "If I say table, you would say _____." (chair)

Prepare sentences similar to those shown below. For oral language exercises, read the sentence, emphasizing the italicized word. One student, or the group in unison, supplies the proper word. For written exercises, students read the sentences and write the missing word.

   1. Please pass the *salt* and _____.
   2. Mother called, "Wear your *hat* and _____."
   3. Before you eat, wash your *face* and _____.
   4. A good breakfast is *bacon* and _____.
   5. We had a snack of *cheese* and _____.
   6. The teacher said, "Get out your *pencil* and _____."
   7. The roads were covered with *snow* and _____.
   8. Dad ordered a cup of coffee with *cream* and _____.
   9. He read the book from *beginning* to _____.
  10. Wash your hands with *soap* and _____.

PROCEDURE: Take away a letter

PURPOSE: To provide practice in working with words.

Directions: The first sentence in each series has one word underlined. Take away a letter from the underlined word to make a new word that will complete the sentence. Continue this for each sentence.

1. Jack likes candy.

    His friend's name is _____.
    Jack _____ Andy are friends.
    They shared _____ apple.
    The boys always have _____ good time.

2. Ted paints a picture.

    Ted likes to _____.
    He cannot paint if he has a _____ in his finger.
    Did he get stuck with a _____?
    Yes, it went _____ his finger!

3. We saw a large boat on the lake.

    The cookies were made with _____ meal.
    I stayed _____ his house yesterday.
    We had _____ good time.

4. Rhode Island is a small state.

    A shopping center is sometimes called a _____.
    _____ of my friends like to go to the shopping center.
    I know a boy whose name is _____.
    He is _____ smart boy.

5. Our flag is sometimes called the Stars and Stripes.

    The top _____ on the flag is red.
    Each stripe is a narrow _____ of color.
    On our _____ we saw many flags displayed.
    A strong wind will sometimes _____ a flag.

6. At the beach he almost stepped on a sun bather.

    The doctor said, "_____ the ankle in hot water."
    After the game Jo took a hot _____.
    A _____ flies around at night.
    The plane leaves _____ six o'clock.

KEY: 1. Andy, and, an, a; 2. paint, pain, pin, in; 3. oat, at, a; 4. mall, all, Al, a; 5. stripe, strip, trip, rip. 6. bathe, bath, bat, at.

PROCEDURE: Provide practice in using letter clues to supply a missing word in a sentence.

Directions:

1. Prepare a series of sentences in which a word is omitted but for which you provide the initial letter.
2. Have the students write a word that keeps the sentence meaningful. In many instances a number of different words may "fit" a particular blank. In the sentences below, answers are given. These should be omitted on prepared seat work.

1. Jerry lost his c_____. (coat, cap, cup, car, cat, etc.)
2. Many enjoyed the b_____ very much. (book, ballgame, boxing, boys, boat, bear, baby)
3. His hobby is r_____. (reading, racing, riding, roping)
4. Beverly went over to Judy's to s_____. (swim, sing, swing, sew, socialize)
5. We all watched the m_____ on television. (man, monkey, movie, monster, meet, match, moon-walk, mobs.)
6. Monday was a very r_____ day. (rainy, rare, rosy, radiant, raw, rough)
7. The children played with the t_____ they had received for Christmas. (toys, tops, trains, trailers, trucks)
8. The teacher dropped the book on my f_____. (foot, finger, fish, flower, feather, flag, folder)

VARIATION: Move from sentences to brief sustained reading passages. In the first exercise below, each missing word must begin with the letter *t*. In the second and third exercises, no letter clue is provided. (Pupils may insert different words. Any combination is acceptable as long as the story makes sense.)

Exercise 1

Gina and Tina are t_____. They like to play with their t_____. One of their favorite toys is a doll named Tammy. T_____ is a t_____ doll and the girls t_____ good care of her.

T_____ can walk and t_____. Gina and Tina often t_____ her to t_____ when they go to shop. Gina and Tina have a t_____ for Tammy's clothes.

The girls have a t_____ also. They t_____ Tammy for a ride on the t_____. Gina and T_____ enjoy T_____ so much it is a t_____ to watch them play with her.
(Key to words left out: twins, toys, Tammy, talking [tall], take, Tammy, talk, take, town, trunk, tricycle, tricycle, Tina, Tammy, thrill [treat].)

Exercise 2

Directions: Complete the following sentences by placing the *same* word in both blank spaces. The word will have different meanings.

1. Leaves _____ from the trees in the _____ of the year.
2. What will we do with the car? We can't _____ it in the _____.
3. Tom _____ a man using a _____ to cut down the tree.
4. A _____ rain caused the river to rise and float the _____ barge off the sand bar.
5. _____ people actually _____ fruits and vegetables at home? Won't they spoil?
6. He told the filling station attendant, "_____ my battery and _____ it to my account."
7. He was the first to set _____ on the _____ of the mountain.
8. Mother said, "if you want the jello to _____, _____ it in the refrigerator."
9. The judges next _____ was "I _____ you to three years in jail."
10. After you chew a _____ of gum, never _____ it under the chair!

Exercise 3

Directions: Fill each blank space with a word that completes the sentence.

1. The score was tied seven to _____.
2. The right hand glove will not fit on your _____ hand.
3. The words *weight* and _____ are called homonyms.
4. A _____ sided figure is called a pentagon.
5. The umpire said, "_____ three, you're out!"
6. Squirrels climb _____ and jump from branch to branch.
7. The world record for running the mile is slightly _____ four minutes.
8. Synonyms are different words that have much the _____ meaning.
9. Washington, D.C. is the _____ of the United States.
10. A _____ that runs on a single track is called a monorail.

PROCEDURE: Read the clue and write a sentence

Directions: Some words have several different meanings. Read the clues provided. Then write sentences using the word so that its meaning in the sentence fits the clue given.

Example:
   save
   a) to rescue: The lifeguard was able to <u>save</u> the swimmer.

   b) accumulate: One should <u>save</u> a part of what he or she earns.

   c) hold for awhile: <u>Save</u> your comments until later.

   d) figurative expression: The losing coach <u>tried to save face</u> by making excuses.

1. **foot**
   a) part of a mountain: _____
   b) a measurement: _____
   c) a figurative expression: _____

2. **broke**
   a) no funds: _____
   b) —a record: _____
   c) illegal entry: _____
   d) figurative expression: _____

3. **light**
   a) not heavy: _____
   b) describes a color: _____
   c) to see with: _____
   d) figurative expression: _____

4. **match**
   a) as in colors: _____
   b) produces flame: _____
   c) —a game: _____

5. **head**
   a) part of body: _____
   b) vegetable: _____
   c) number of cattle: _____
   d) figurative expression: _____

6. **bank**
   a) river: _____
   b) funds: _____
   c) an "expression": _____

Interpreting Proverbs

PURPOSE: To provide opportunities for students to interpret proverbs.

Students were asked to write what they thought certain proverbs mean. Although they each read the same sentences their interpretations were quite varied. A few examples are provided.

1. *If life gives you lemons, make lemonade.*
   1. "It means don't go around feeling sorry for yourself."
   2. "Although lemonade is bitter, it is good for you."
   3. "Life is not going to be a bed of roses."
   4. "Make the most of all your opportunities."
   5. "Each cloud has a silver lining, if you can find it."

2. *Money is a good servant, but a poor master.*
   1. "Money should be put to good uses, not hoarded."
   2. "Money won't buy happiness."
   3. "If you want to acquire more and more money, you will never be happy with what you have."
   4. "It's true that money talks but you don't have to listen."

3. *Each snowflake in an avalanche pleads not guilty.*
   1. "Why should it plead guilty, no one snowflake started the avalanche."
   2. "Men act out in a mob what they think in silence."
   3. "A snowflake is clean, white and pure, all symbols for being not guilty."
   4. "When the avalanche comes, snowflakes act like people."
   5. "No one (not even a snowflake) wants to assume any blame for tragedy."

4. *A giraffe is a horse put together by a committee.*
   1. "This is not true, so it tells us not to believe everything we read."
   2. "Most committees have trouble making decisions."
   3. "I haven't the slightest idea what it means."
   4. "It's like 'too many cooks spoil the soup.' "

Directions: Read each of the following proverbs and then write what it means to you.

1. A chain is as strong as its weakest link.

   _____

   _____

   _____

2. It is easier to forgive an enemy than a friend.

   _____

   _____

   _____

3. A journey of a thousand miles begins with a single step.

   _____

   _____

   _____

4. People are lonely because they build walls instead of bridges.

   _____

   _____

   _____

5. One great use of words is to hide our thoughts.

   _____

   _____

   _____

6. He who teaches me for a day is my father for a lifetime.

   _____

   _____

   _____

7. The devil can quote scripture for his purpose.

   _____

   _____

   _____

8. Character is what you are when no one is watching

   _____

   _____

   _____

VARIATION: Explain the nature of proverbs. They are brief statements that are widely used which seem to reflect great wisdom. They are quoted time and again because they are brief and pithy. However, this virtue can also cause problems of interpretation, since the meaning is not spelled out.

Directions: "Write what each proverb means to you." (When exercise is completed, be sure that students get to hear various interpretations.)

1. Don't let your studies get in the way of your learning.

   _____

   _____

2. He who pays the fiddler, calls the tune.

   _____

   _____

3. The early bird gets the worm.

   _____

   _____

4. A journey of a 1000 miles begins with a single step.

   _____

   _____

VARIATION: Sometimes a proverb fits a certain situation and would not be good advice all the time. Statements **A** and **B** below seem to give different advice.

Directions: Describe a situation where **A** is good advice. Then do the same for statement **B**.

   A. He who hesitates is lost.
   B. Always look before you leap.

   A. When one door is shut, another is opened.
   B. Opportunity knocks but once.

   A. Many hands make light work.
   B. Too many cooks spoil the broth.

Directions: If statements **A** and **B** have the same meaning write **S** in the box. If the meanings are opposite write **O.**

1. **A.** Absence makes the heart grow fonder.
   B. Out of sight is out of mind.

2. **A.** You can't unscramble eggs.
   B. No use crying over spilled milk.

3. **A.** Rather be ignorant of a matter than half know it.
   B. A little learning is a dangerous thing.

4. **A.** Experience is the name everyone gives to his mistakes.
   B. Experience is the best teacher.

5. **A.** He who hesitates is lost.
   B. Make haste slowly.

VARIATION: Matching proverbs

Directions: In the box there is one statement that has much the same meaning as one of the numbered statements beneath the box. Write **A, B, C,** or **D** in front of the numbered statement that has the same meaning.

> A. Hindsight is often better than foresight.
> B. Never put off 'till tomorrow what you can do today.
> C. Birds of a feather flock together.
> D. Different strokes for different folks.

_____ 1. You can know a man by the company he keeps.
_____ 2. One man's meat is another man's poison.
_____ 3. After the event, even a fool is wise.
_____ 4. Make hay while the sun shines.

Reading, Writing, and Dramatization

Integrating reading and writing activities is one of the best ways to help students understand how their language works. Instruction can ignore labels for parts of speech and other such rules, and students will still learn syntax by combining and expanding sentences and rewriting scrambled word orders.

Students will note the inherent logic of language usage when they arrange sentences into meaningful paragraphs. They can become aware of the precision that can be achieved with language when they attempt to write directions for simple activities such as playing Hop-Scotch, Tic Tac Toe, or how to get from school to the nearest hospital or fire station.

Learners discover that what they write actually becomes reading and that they can improve their reading ability by reading what they and their friends have written. Working with language is highly motivating and the reading—writing activities can focus on children's interests. Their interests can then lead to reading the more conventional materials that the school cherishes so highly.

Working with oral language leads to important insights relative to the power, flexibility, and precision of language. Students note that gaining precision with language is a long-term process, not something that is mastered with one exercise. However, they also note that they can start the process now! Learning to describe how a paper clip works is part of the continuum that eventually leads to explaining how a jet engine works or how to perform heart surgery.

Combining Sentences

PROCEDURE: Using materials such as shown below, illustrate on the chalkboard how two or more sentences may be combined. Prepare exercises which children can do as seat work.

TEACHER: "Combine each series of sentences into one sentence."

1. Nancy has a new coat.
   Her mother bought it for her.

   _____

2. John has a dog.
   It is a collie.
   It is a friendly dog.

   _____

3. I have a bicycle.
   It is painted green and white.
   My brother gave it to me.

   _____

4. Cindy is a dog.
   She is a cocker spaniel.
   Her hair is brown.

   _____

5. Mary found a frog.
   It was little.
   The frog hopped and hopped.

   _____

6. Fred has a toy.
   It is new.
   His mother gave it to him.
   It is an airplane.

   _____

Example of responses

1. Nancy's mother bought her a new coat.
2. John has a friendly collie dog. (John's dog is a friendly collie.)
3. My brother gave me a green and white bicycle. (I have a green and white bicycle that my brother gave to me.)
4. Cindy is a brown cocker spaniel.
5. Mary found a little frog that hopped and hopped.
6. Fred's mother gave him a new toy airplane. (Fred has a new toy airplane that his mother gave to him.)

Expanding Sentences

In the hands of a skilled teacher, this activity will probably result in as much pupil growth "per time unit invested" as will any activity in the school curriculum. One should not conclude that this type of experience relates primarily to learning to write. Children learn much about language and the melody of language which must be incorporated into reading. The less emphasis there is on grammatical labels, the more the child will learn about the word patterns (syntax) that English sentences will accommodate.

PROCEDURE:

1. Start with any kernel sentence.

John has a dog.

Point out that this does not tell us much about the dog and invite children to suggest one or more words that tells us what kind of a dog John has.
(Breed)   John has a *boxer* dog.
(In succession, deal with size, color, characteristics, etc.)
(Size)   John has a *big,* boxer dog.
(Color)   John has a big, *brown,* boxer dog.
(Characteristic)   John has a *friendly,* big, brown, boxer dog.
(Who is John?)   John, my brother. . . .
            John, my friend. . . .
            John, the man who runs the newsstand. . . .
Sentences can "fit" any grade or academic level. Variations are unlimited since the activity may be oral, written, or a combination of both. Chalkboard work provides excellent opportunities to teach punctuation facts.
2. Demonstrate different word patterns for the same message.

My brother John has a big, brown, friendly, boxer.
The big, friendly, brown, boxer dog belongs to my brother, John.

VARIATION: Add one word (or phrase) at a time to each of the following sentences. You may add the words any place in the sentence.

1. Birds fly.
2. The boys were playing.
3. Jane has a sister.
4. The picnic was fun.

Gobbledygook

PURPOSE: The purpose of the following exercises is not to teach children to write or respect gobbledygook. However, playing "language games" can help them understand and detect this type of language usage when they meet it. Also, this type of experience can lead to respect for "a sentence that packs in the meaning."

A little material similar to the following could be used to introduce the exercises:

The term *gob • le • de • gook* was invented by a politician from Texas. He used it to describe long winded speeches that "beat around the bush" and sounded like turkey talk. (Yes! The term is in the dictionary.) Gobbledygook is use of language that is almost the opposite of the language found in proverbs. A proverb is brief, pithy, and full of meaning. Gobbledygook is a lot of words—a use of language to cover up meaning.

Example: *Gobbledygook*: "Don't trade or barter your trusty steed for another when you are in the act of negotiating a body of moving water."
          Proverb: "Don't trade horses in the middle of the stream."

Directions: Each of the following lengthy statements says the same thing as a short pithy proverb you have probably heard. Write the proverb below the statement.

1. If you sew a little rip in the garment before it gets torn into a big hole, you will save a lot of work. _____
2. The writing device that employs ink is often more powerful than the sharp-bladed hand weapon. _____
3. A recently acquired implement for brushing away floor dirt, will likely remove the dirt efficiently. _____
4. The winged creature that is up and hopping about early in the day, will be the one that secures its breakfast. _____
5. One cannot devour the sweet, bread like dessert with icing, and also save it for a rainy day. _____

Interpreting Turkey Talk:

Directions: Match a gobbledygook statement under **A,** with a proverb under **B.** Write the number of the proverb in front of the statement that has the same meaning.

A

_____ If a fanged canine is in peaceful repose, do not agitate it into restlessness.

_____ When early efforts do not bear fruit, persist in thy endeavors.

_____ The turf beyond the border invariably seems to be of deeper hue than that which is near by.

_____ A group of culinary experts will have a bad effect on the production of tasty soup.

_____ He who seeks his bed prior to the customary time for doing so, and who arouses himself at dawn's first light, will surely be robust and be blessed with riches and wisdom.

B

Note: One of the following proverbs will not be used above.

1. Too many cooks spoil the broth.
2. Look before you leap!
3. Early to bed and early to rise, makes a man healthy, wealthy and wise.
4. If at first you don't succeed, try, try again.
5. The grass is always greener on the other side of the fence.
6. Let sleeping dogs lie.

Directions: Translate these proverbs into gobbledygook.

1. Birds of a feather flock together.

   _____
   _____
   _____

2. A good start is half the race.

   _____
   _____
   _____

Picture Stories

PROCEDURE:

1. Provide snapshots of individual pupils. Children then write a biography or a story about themselves and paste the photograph on the title page.
2. Provide snapshots of some school activities (book fair, Halloween costume party, parents' visitation, science fair). Children use snapshots to illustrate individually or group-produced stories about the event depicted.
3. Gather news pictures which need not be related to the immediate school surroundings (famous athletes, pollution scene, television series, visit to community or area by a famous person, etc.). Children write stories using pictures to heighten interest.

Examples:

Pupils' Photo	School Activity Photo

This is Mary.

Our School Christmas Party

Picture Sequence

Trace a series of pictures which suggest a story. Child composes the story, orally or written.

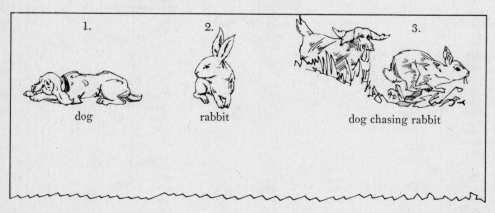

1. dog 2. rabbit 3. dog chasing rabbit

PROCEDURE: Gather interesting pictures and paste each of them on a card or page. Children are instructed to "write a story about the picture." When the pictures are somewhat vague, the writer must "provide the context."

Write a story about this picture.

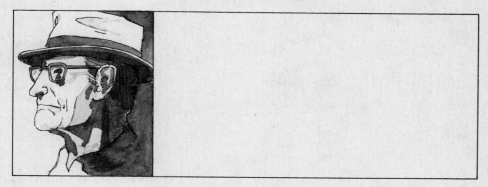

"We interrupt this program to bring you the following news bulletin" (Write the news story).

Finish the story: "In this picture the people are. . . . "

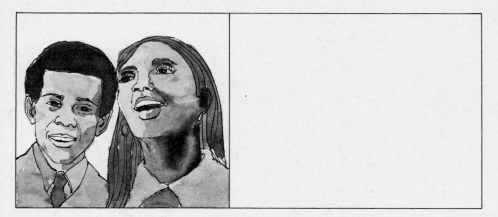

Write a title for this picture. Then write the story.

When I look at this picture I think of . . .

Write a story about this picture.

Who is this? What is she thinking?

Building Paragraphs

PROCEDURE: Place five or more related facts on the chalkboard or on 3 X 5 cards. Pupils are to write a paragraph which includes all of the facts given.

Teacher: "Write a paragraph that includes all of the facts given."

Washington Monument

located in Washington, D.C.
completed in 1884
hollow inside
contains elevator
walls are fifteen feet thick at bottom

555 feet tall
can go to top by steps
elevator trip is seventy seconds
took over four years to build
contains 898 steps

Apollo 13

three astronauts on board
blasted off April 8, 1970
power failure 200,000 miles from earth
many stages
dangerous return trip
in space for three days

destination moon
had to fly the "Lem"
very cold inside ship
national appeal for prayers for safe return
darkness inside ship
landed safely

Brazil

language spoken is Portuguese
Amazon River is in Brazil
coffee, bananas, and sugar grow there
coffee is the major export
capital city is Brasilia

gold and diamonds are found in Brazil
largest nation in South America
industries are mining and cotton weaving
south central region has the best climate

The White House

In 1814 there was a fire and it was rebuilt
the address is 1600 Pennsylvania Avenue
the White House is located in Washington, D.C.
Jacqueline Kennedy supervised restoration of several rooms
it was rebuilt again in 1952

completed when John Adams was president
in 1817 it was painted white
home of the President of the United States
today it has 107 rooms and 31 bathrooms
approximately one million people visit it each year

Writing Descriptions

PURPOSE: To provide practice in observing and writing descriptions of familiar objects, reports, directions for playing games, and definitions of terms used in sports.

Describing One's Surroundings

PROCEDURE: Prepare several sheets of paper with instructions for writing descriptions of various familiar items.

Example: Write a description of:

your classroom
the person sitting to your right
your bicycle
the neighborhood where you live

our school building
lunch time in the cafeteria
school buses loading and leaving
after school
the playground during recess (or
before school starts)

Writing Directions and Definitions

PROCEDURE: It is difficult to write concise descriptions for playing simple games, giving directions, or explaining terms from sports. Have children carry out the following writing tasks and read their descriptions to the class. Encourage the listeners to ask questions which focus on omissions or confusing statements.

TEACHER: "Write the directions for the following:"

playing hop scotch
playing tic tac toe
playing Capture the Flag, Musical Chairs, Drop the Handkerchief, Red Rover, Stick Ball, Hide and Seek, or other games children play
finding a book in the library
going from the school to the fire station (bus station, park, or any nearby building in the neighborhood)
walking from this classroom to the cafeteria (or library, gym, etc.)

TEACHER: "Write an explanation of any of the following sports terms."

Football	Basketball	Tennis
Safety	Traveling	Set
Illegal Procedure	Zone Defense	Love
Screen Pass	Pivot	Mixed Doubles
Clipping	Technical foul	Game
On-side Kick	Screen	Double Fault

Sentence Production

PURPOSE: To help students write several sentences using a limited number of words.

PROCEDURE: Select four, five, six, or seven words that can be arranged in various sentence patterns. Print each word on a separate card and place the cards in an envelope. Have children work individually or in pairs. Direct them to select an envelope, arrange the words into a sentence, write the sentence, and continue to rearrange the words into other sentences, writing down each sentence. Each word must be used—but only once, no words can be added or changed in any way.

Example: listen   speak   I   you   when

  1.   when   you   speak   I   listen
  2. You listen when I speak.
  3. When you listen I speak.
  4. I listen when you speak.
  5. I speak when you listen.
  6. When I listen, you speak.
  7. You speak when I listen.
  8. When I speak, you listen.
  9. You! When I speak, listen!

Using the words on each line, write as many different sentences as you can.

  1. Joe   talks   while   Jim   walks
  2. A   tall   building   is   a   skyscraper
  3. He   does   what   she   says

PROCEDURE: The following demonstrates how a great number of sentences can be developed using a limited number of words. In this instance, punctuation and intonation play a major role.

The doctor said his friend is ill.

1. His friend said, is the doctor ill?
2. "The doctor," said his friend, "is ill."
3. Said the doctor, "His friend is ill."
4. His friend said, "The doctor is ill."
5. "His friend," said the doctor, "is ill."
6. The doctor said, "Is his friend ill?"
7. "Is his friend ill?", said the doctor.
8. The doctor is ill, said his friend.
9. "Is the doctor," said his friend, "ill?"
10. Said the doctor, "Is his friend ill?"
11. "Is the doctor ill?", said his friend.
12. Said his friend, "The doctor is ill."
13. The doctor said, "His friend is ill."
14. "His friend is ill," said the doctor.
15. Said his friend, "Is the doctor ill?"
16. His doctor said, "The friend is ill."
17. "His doctor," said the friend, "is ill."
18. "His friend," said the doctor, "is ill."
19. Is the said doctor his ill friend?
20. The doctor is ill? said his friend.

On your own, make up a short sentence that can be rearranged into many different sentences. If your first attempt doesn't work—try again.

Oral Language Activities

RATIONALE: Students need opportunities for using oral language in speaking to groups. These must go beyond mere recitation in the various content areas. There are hundreds of activities which can enhance the creative use of language, many of which parallel real life situations. Such activities can consist of brief presentations which focus on organization, and the use of logic, persuasion, and precision in language. Each can be adapted to individual presentations or involve pairs of students or small groups. A few illustrations follow.

The Way It Might Have Been

PROCEDURE: The narrator starts with any myth, fairy tale or classic story. However, only the title and introductory material are retained. At a given point in the story, the narrator shifts the plot and outcome in any way desired.

Examples: 1. Goldilocks finds that she can talk to the bears. She invites them to join her in a television series in which they are a typical bear family who adopt Goldilocks. In one episode they all become ecology wardens and track down villains who pollute streams or who carelessly start forest fires; or, they could mount a crusade against zoos which keep wild animals penned up.

2. Romeo and Juliet launch a campaign to make adults (their families) act in a rational manner. They plan a big party and see to it that both families attend. At the party they announce their plans to be married. Arguments ensue, but love triumphs.

Introductions and Interviews

PROCEDURE: This activity involves pairs of students. One participant plays the role of any well-known national figure such as a movie star, sports figure or politician, or a well-known local individual such as a school principal, mayor, bus driver, disc jockey, etc.

The other participant introduces and interviews this celebrity. This can be a rehearsed production, or an impromptu ad-lib session.

Show and Tell (with a twist)

PROCEDURE:

1. A child describes a common object (pencil, paper clip, bobby pin, scissors, etc.). He or she works from the assumption that no one in the group has ever seen or heard of the object, and explains the object's design, material, function, etc. When the student is finished, the others in the class or group ask questions about the object.

Illustration (child describing a pencil): "This is a pencil. It is used for writing. The outside is made of wood which you see is painted yellow. Inside the wood is a long piece of lead. You cut away the wood and then the lead writes on paper."

Questions: The pencil you showed is round. Are all pencils round? Are all pencils yellow? Are pencils always the same length as the one you showed? What's that metal strip near one end of the pencil? Explain the end that doesn't write (eraser), etc.

2. After several of these sessions the teacher can show a common object that has not been discussed. Each pupil writes out the complete explanation of this object. (ruler, envelope, Scotch tape, box of crayons, a sheet of paper, a stapler, etc.)

VARIATION: Use a group approach. One first grade teacher reported that she had a "nonverbal group," so perhaps this approach might not work for her. However, she tried the procedure of "let's find out what we know about paper bags." She provided three or four different types of bags—a very small candy bag, an insulated bag used for frozen foods, a large grocery bag, and a shopping bag. She recorded the responses given by children which resulted in three typewritten pages! ("bags hold things"— "carry things in them"—"they won't hold liquids"—"yes they do, you can put milk in them"—"first, the milk has to be in a carton"—"the ice cream won't melt very fast"— "bags come in all sizes"—"shopping bags have handles," etc.) She learned that the children were not nonverbal.

Add a Word

PROCEDURE: Prepare a number of cards, each containing a kernel sentence (*Birds fly, John has a dog* (see p. 89). One sentence is selected and written on the chalkboard. Each successive participant adds one word (or phrase). This word can be inserted anywhere in the sentence providing it "fits" or meets the test of English syntax.

Teams may compete, using the same stimulus sentence, in attempting to develop the longest sentence.

Add a Sentence

This activity can involve pairs of students, small groups, or the entire class.

PROCEDURE: The first participant introduces a story by relating one or two sentences. The next participant adds one sentence. Each successive participant adds one sentence. The objective is to add material that will permit the story to continue.

VARIATION: At a given point, the oral presentation would be terminated and each student would write a one paragraph conclusion to the story.

Telephone Barter

PROCEDURE: Prepare a series of cards, each containing a "for sale" or "wanted" ad.

Examples:

for sale: Ten speed bike, limited use, good condition.

for sale: Parakeet and cage. Bird sings! Moving, must sell.

wanted: Old comic books, science, monster supers, etc.

Two participants select a card. One plays the role of seller, the other is the potential buyer. The buyer raises questions, seller answers them and extols the virtues of the item. A time limit of one (or two) minutes can be imposed for each transaction.

Memory Chain I

PURPOSE: Develops listening and oral language skills.

PROCEDURE: Teacher starts a story by providing the initial sentence.

Teacher: "John went to the store and bought milk and bread."
             Volunteers are then called upon to say (in proper sequence) the items
             John purchased.
Child (1):   "Milk and bread."
Teacher: "John bought milk, bread, and potatoes."
Child (2):   "Milk, bread, and potatoes."
Teacher: "John bought milk, bread, potatoes, and rice."
Child (3):   (Continue to optimum number of items for group.)

VARIATIONS: When the game is terminated, all children are to write all items mentioned: (1) in order presented; (2) in any order (easier task). This game can also be played by two, three, four or more children in a group.

Memory Chain II

PURPOSE: Develops listening and oral language skills.

PROCEDURE: Prepare a series of cards, each of which contains a typed message. Each card is placed in a separate envelope. (Alternative approach: Record the messages on tape.) One child reads (or listens to tape). He then tells the second child the message. This child repeats the message to the third child, etc. (A cycle may include four or five children.) The last child in the cycle repeats the message to the group, each of whom compares this message with the original. The group then discusses the modifications that have occurred.

VARIATION: When appropriate for group, each member of the chain tells the next member the message and then immediately writes it down. Comparisons of written messages will help to point up where the changes occurred. (As a general rule, this activity need not focus on spelling of words.)

Sample Messages:

1. Mrs. Charles Brown will visit our class tomorrow at 9:30 in the morning. She will tell us about national parks. She will show pictures of several parks including Yellowstone and the Grand Canyon.
2. A red fox was seen yesterday evening near the edge of Riverside Park. The fox was reported by Mrs. James Rogers who lives nearby. Mr. Williams, a game warden, said that sighting the fox in that area was quite unusual.

Impromptu Oral Stories

PURPOSE: To allow students to project meaning into a picture.

PROCEDURE: Secure a number of pictures similar to those found on pages 92 to 95. Pictures should not show individuals who might be easily recognized such as the president, well known political or sports figures. Also, students should not have studied those pictures prior to their use. The pictures should be somewhat vague in order to permit different interpretations. Place pictures face down. A student then selects one picture and is permitted to study it for ten seconds. The picture is then displayed to the audience while the narrator tells a story about the picture. When the storyteller has finished, anyone in the audience who has a different interpretation may volunteer to tell his or her version. The storyteller selects one volunteer. This process can be repeated.

How Alike? How Different?

PURPOSE: To provide experience in critical thinking and oral expression.

PROCEDURE: Prepare a number of stimulus cards, each of which contains the names of two things. Students draw a card, read the stimulus words to the group, and then tell how these are *alike* and how they are *different*.

Examples:

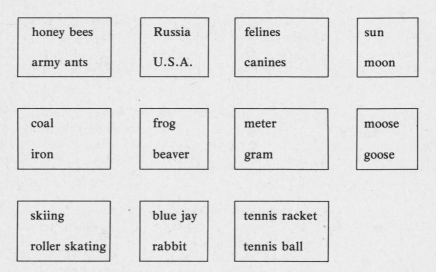

honey bees army ants	Russia U.S.A.	felines canines	sun moon
coal iron	frog beaver	meter gram	moose goose
skiing roller skating	blue jay rabbit	tennis racket tennis ball	

VARIATION: After the speaker has concluded, permit listeners to volunteer to tell other ways in which the two things are the same or different.

Giving Directions

PROCEDURE: Give directions for doing something that is fairly simple, but do not use any terms that will reveal the objective. For example, give directions for drawing a square, but do not use the term square.

1. Draw a straight line that is twelve inches long. The line must be parallel to the top of the chalkboard.
2. At the right end of the line, draw a twelve inch line straight down.
3. At the bottom of this line, draw a line twelve inches to the left. This line must be parallel to the top of the chalkboard.
4. At the left end of this line, draw a twelve inch line straight up to meet with the left end of the first line drawn.

PROCEDURE: Prepare a number of cards, each of which contains a task for giving directions.

Examples:

Give the directions for playing Tic-Tac-Toe.

Give the directions for walking from the school to the public library.

Give the directions for folding an 8" x 11" sheet of paper into an airplane.

Give directions for writing a Haiku poem.

Give the directions for passing the examination for a driver's license.

The participant draws a card and gives the directions called for. The listeners attempt to identify errors, omissions, or any statements that might be vague or misleading.

Minute Media Messages

PROCEDURE: Prepare a number of task cards, each of which describes an activity that would be performed by a radio or television announcer. Participants select a card and prepare a one minute presentation on the topic identified on the card.

Examples:

1. The Sixty Second Pitch.
   Each card contains the directions: "You are a radio (or T.V.) announcer. Present a commercial in which you sell _____. (see list of possible products). Perhaps you can develop a slogan with a punch. You must create a demand for the product."

   Possible products for the sixty second pitch:
   used cars
   Foxy Popsie—The sweet new drink, bottles or cans.
   Amalgamated Albatross Airlines (up and away with triple A?)
   The *U*ltimate *S*uper *S*peed *R*eading Course (USSR). Enroll today.
   karate
   Dolce • derm Lotion—Buy Dolce • derm and you have sweet skin.

2. Micro Newscasts
   "And now the weather. . . . "
   "We interrupt this broadcast for the following news bulletin:"
   "The Wall Street update . . . Today's market"
   "We're down to the final minute of this exciting contest. The score is tied. . . . (Make up the final minute broadcast of a basketball, football, hockey, etc. game).
   "Highlights from the president's "talk to the people." . . .

Dramatization

Acting Out Proverbs

PURPOSE: This activity provides children the opportunity to dramatize or pantomime such familiar proverbs as: *If the shoe fits, wear it, Don't cry over spilled milk, Speak softly and carry a big stick.*

PROCEDURE: Prepare a number of cards, each containing one well-known proverb. Give several individuals (or teams) the same proverb and have them independently work out interpretations. The individuals, or teams, act out the proverb. The rest of the class guesses which is being dramatized.

Illustration: Items for individual interpretations:
>   Two heads are better than one.
>   Hindsight is often better than foresight.
>   Never look a gift horse in the mouth.
>   If at first you don't succeed, try again.
>   You can lead a horse to water, but you can't make it drink.
>   Make hay while the sun shines.
>   The pen is mightier than the sword.
>   One picture is worth a thousand words.
>   Look before you leap.
>   Don't speak out of both sides of your mouth.

Items for pairs of students, or small teams:
>   A chain is no stronger than its weakest link.
>   Three may keep a secret if two of them are dead.
>   Different folks use different strokes.
>   Too many cooks spoil the broth.
>   Never swap horses in the middle of the stream.
>   An apple a day keeps the doctor away.
>   He who laughs last, laughs best.
>   Many hands make light work.
>   Birds of a feather, flock together.
>   If a man does not keep pace with his companions, perhaps it is because he hears a different drummer.

Acting Out Directions

PROCEDURE:

1. Prepare a number of 3 X 5 cards, each of which contains a one sentence set of directions.
2. Explain to the children that they are to act out the task silently. (Pantomime.)
3. Volunteers select a card, read the directions silently, and perform the activity described.

Examples of Activities:

Act like you are rowing a boat.
You are the pitcher in a baseball game.
Pretend you are sharpening a pencil.
You are the cheerleader at a basketball game.
All the seats are full when you get on the bus.
You are getting a "shot" in the doctor's office.
You put a coin in the milk machine—and it doesn't work.

PARTICIPATION:

Entire class.
Smaller group, or several groups working simulataneously.
Two teams competing: one child from Team A performs, members of Team B guess the activity. Alternate this procedure; the team with the fewest guesses wins.
Pairs of children (procedure same as teams).

PROCEDURE: For junior thespians

You are . . .

a surgeon performing an operation
playing chess with the champion
judging a beauty contest
sculpturing clay (shaping a head)
a clerk selling men's suits (you have two customers!)
operating a huge crane (building a skyscraper)
a door-to-door salesperson selling _____ (you name it)
watching: a car race on an oval track
          a tennis match
          a diving contest

An Old Myth

PROCEDURE: Explain that you are going to tell a story in which there are three characters—

> a very poor woodcutter
> his wife
> a fish with magical powers

After you tell the story, the class will be divided up into "casts of three." Each group of three pupils will act out the story using their own words.

The story:

The woodcutter and his wife were very poor. One day the woodcutter went fishing. He caught a fine fish, and he thought how good it would taste for dinner.

Just then the fish spoke to him and said, "I have magical powers and if you will put me back in the water, I will grant the first three wishes that either you or your good wife ask."

The man decided that the three wishes would be better than eating the fish. So he put the fish back in the water. He hurried home and told his wife about the fish and what it had promised. The wife said he was very foolish to let the fish go.

The woodcutter was very hungry and pretty soon he said, "I wish we had a nice fish all prepared and ready to eat." Instantly, there appeared on the table a fine fish.

His wife saw this and shouted, "Look, you have wasted a wish—I wish that fish were on the end of your nose." Immediately the fish became attached to his nose and the poor woodcutter could not get it off. Finally, he said, "My, I wish I could get this fish off my nose." The fish was now back on the table.

FOLLOW UP: After the children have acted out the story, change the game so that each child can write out the wishes he or she would make if he or she were granted three wishes.

Study
Skills

Good instruction should equip students to become more and more independent in searching out and acquiring knowledge. To be able to assume responsibility for their own intellectual growth, children must master a number of study skills.

Included among study skills are locating, evaluating, organizing, summarizing, and retaining information. In addition to these skills, students must gradually become more efficient in reading. This particular skill is often discussed under the headings of rate or flexibility. Good readers develop efficient reading habits. They do not read one word at a time; they combine words into thought units, and they can and do read different materials at different rates.

The need for efficient study skills increases as pupils advance through the grades. While they are needed in every curricular area, these skills may not be systematically taught in any of the curriculum areas simply because they are not part of the "content."

Our schools are often criticized for relying too much on textbooks. One of the reasons that the use of these materials is often quite inefficient, however, is because children have not learned how to "mine" a book. Many students do not profit from the reader's aids found in texts, such as the preface, index, table of contents, glossary, appendix, tables and illustrations, and the like. The materials that follow focus on a number of important study skills ranging from dictionary usage to improving rate of reading.

Working With Dictionary Skills

Alphabetizing

PURPOSE: To provide practice in arranging a series of items in alphabetical order.

TEACHER: "Words in a dictionary are listed in alphabetical order. In each line of words below, put a number in front of each word to show which would come first in the dictionary, which would come second, and which would come third."

Example: __3__ cart   __1__ ant   __2__ ball

1. __ animal   __ camel   __ dog
2. __ rabbit   __ mule   __ tiger
3. __ goat   __ snake   __ deer
4. __ river   __ boat   __ jump
5. __ farm   __ form   __ fish
6. __ stove   __ sink   __ saw
7. __ pig   __ pit   __ pin
8. __ gate   __ game   __ coat

TEACHER: "Study the words in the box and write them in alphabetical order."

knot	knee	knob	knit
knife	knock	knight	know

1. _____   5. _____
2. _____   6. _____
3. _____   7. _____
4. _____   8. _____

absent	abound	abroad	above
about	absolute	able	

1. _____   5. _____
2. _____   6. _____
3. _____   7. _____
4. _____   8. _____

TEACHER: "In each of the following series, use the author's last name to list the items in alphabetical order. Place the number 1 in front of the item that would be first, the number 2 in front of the second item, etc."

_____ Felton, Harold W., *Big Mose: Hero Fireman*
_____ Deleeuw, Adele, *Paul Bunyan Finds a Wife*
_____ Shapiro, Edna, *Windwagon Smith*
_____ Caudill, Rebecca, *A Certain Small Shepherd*
_____ Tarkington, Booth, *Penrod*

_____ Clark, Leonard, *Flutes and Cymbals*
_____ Dejong, Meindert, *Journey from Peppermint Street*
_____ Neufeld, John, *Edgar Allen*
_____ Nyblom, Helena, *The Witch of the Woods*
_____ Northrup, Mili, *The Watch Cat*

_____ Buckley, Helen E., *The Little Pig in the Cupboard*
_____ Shannon, Terry, and Payzant, Charles, *The Sea Searchers*
_____ Hess, Lilo, *The Curious Raccoon*
_____ Buck, Margaret W., *Where They Go in Winter*
_____ Freeman, Mae, *The Book of Magnets*

_____ Burch, Robert, *Queenie Peavy*
_____ Blackburn, Joyce, *Martha Berry*
_____ Bailey, Bernadine, *Picture Book of Georgia*
_____ Burchard, Peter, *Bimby*
_____ Berrill, Jacqueline, *Wonders of Animal Nurseries*

TEACHER: "Read the following authors and titles carefully and number them in alphabetical order. Remember, the author's last name is the key."

_____ *The Little Girl and the Tiny Doll,* by Edward and Aingelda Ardizzone
_____ *The Piemakers,* by Helen Cresswell
_____ *The Battle of St. George Without,* by Janet McNeill
_____ *The Foolish Bird,* by Henri Maik
_____ *The Longest Name on the Block,* by Jane Yolen
_____ *Pass to Win: Pro Football Greats,* by George Sullivan
_____ *The Snow Firing,* by Joyce Gard
_____ *Tall Sails to Jamestown,* by Eugenia Stone
_____ *The High King,* by Lloyd Alexander

Use of Guide Words

TEACHER: "The top of each page in the dictionary contains two guide words. The word at the left of the page is the first word on the page, and the word on the right is the last word on the page."

Example: Circle the words below which you would not find on a page if the guide words are **row** and **ruby**.

rubber	royal
run	rub
ruffle	rudder
row	rube

Circle the words you would not find on a page if guide words are **sidewise** and **signet**.

silent	siding
siesta	sight
sign	signature
signal	silk

TEACHER: Assume that each of the following words are found on one dictionary page. Which of the words would be the guide words?

Guide words: _____   _____

breakable	breaker
breakfast	breeze
break	breed
breath	breezy

Guide words: _____   _____

florist	flue
Florida	fluffy
flower	flour
flow	flown

Estimating Location of Words

PURPOSE: To facilitate use of a dictionary without tabs. To provide practice in entering the dictionary near the point where the desired word is located.

PROCEDURE: Discuss how the dictionary can be divided roughly into halves, A—M and N—Z, and into four sections, A—E, F—M, N—S, and T—Z. Pronounce a list of words and have the children open their dictionaries as close as possible to the word you have pronounced.

Examples: chair (section 1)   tin (section 4)
           doorstep (section 1)   gate (section 2)
           record (section 3)   zoo (section 4)
           neighbor (section 2)   queen (section 3)

PROCEDURE: Mark four boxes with the four sections of the alphabet: A—E, F—M, N—S, T—Z. Write words on separate cards for each section of the alphabet. Place the cards in the appropriate boxes. Have students select a box, take out the cards, and arrange them in alphabetical order. The student may also write the words in alphabetical order. The difficulty of this exercise is determined by the number of cards used.

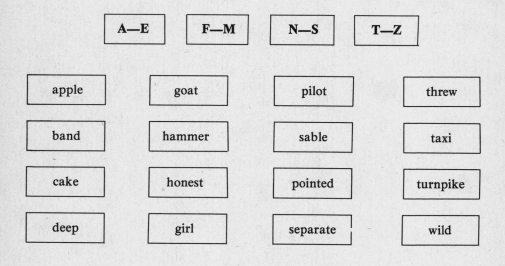

Using the Dictionary for Word Meanings

PROCEDURE: Duplicate a page of sentences each of which contains one underlined word. Beneath each sentence, have the children write as many synonyms as they can for the underlined word. Encourage use of the dictionary.

1. That house has been <u>vacant</u> for many years.

   _____

2. The mean queen had no <u>affection</u> for Snow White.

   _____

3. The explorers were looking for someone to <u>guide</u> them up the mountain.

   _____

4. The child was very <u>timid</u>.

   _____

5. The teacher was <u>upset</u> with the class.

   _____

6. Grandfather read them a very <u>exciting</u> story.

   _____

7. They were <u>happy</u> to hear the good news.

   _____

8. It was a very <u>generous</u> offer.

   _____

9. The girls kept their room very <u>neat</u>.

   _____

10. The law does not <u>permit</u> parking here.

    _____

Dictionary Maze

PROCEDURE: Set up a number of areas in the classroom for studying the following dictionary skills.

1. list of words to alphabetize
   a. first letters the same
   b. first two letters the same
   c. first three letters the same
   d. all initial letters different
2. list of book titles to alphabetize
3. list of author's names to alphabetize

How to "Mine" a Book

PURPOSE: To provide experiences which lead children to a better understanding of how to use the various helps provided in most textbooks. (Examples: table of contents, index, glossary)

PROCEDURE:

1. Select any textbook (social studies, science, math).
2. Write a number of sentences, each of which will lead the learner to use one of the aids to learning found in the book.
3. A duplicated work sheet may be used with the class as a whole, then with small groups and individual pupils for review.

TEACHER: "Use your textbook to answer the following questions and to complete the sentences." (Some of the information in the sentences below will need to be changed to correspond with the textbooks your class is using.)

1. The index begins on page _____ and ends on page _____.
2. List three types of information found in the appendix:

   _____   _____   _____
3. What key word do we look under if we wish information on Bonneville? _____   Grand Coulee and Hoover dams? _____
4. What page contains the populations and capitals of each state? _____
5. What page of your book has a picture of a *blockhouse* (use the index)? _____
6. Under the heading *Civil War,* you are told to see another heading. What is it? _____
7. How many subtopics are listed under the entry *Great Ideas?* _____
8. Are each of these listed somewhere else in the index? _____
9. Pages 482–492 are called an *atlas.* Study these pages; then write a definition of the term *atlas.*
10. Where do you find the definition of erosion? _____
11. On what page do you find data telling you which state has the largest and which the smallest area? _____
12. On what page will you find a picture showing erosion? _____
13. What is the pronunciation of *Sault St. Marie?* _____
14. Does your book contain a diagram showing how plywood is made? _____
15. Page _____ contains a list of all of the maps found in the book.

Using the Encyclopedia

PURPOSE: To provide an understanding of the encyclopedia as a resource tool and to provide practice in its efficient use.

PROCEDURE:

1. Duplicate a drawing that represents the various volumes in an encyclopedia set. (Show volume number and alphabetical coverage.)
2. Ask students to identify the volume that would contain data on certain topics. Discussion should focus on the importance of selecting the proper heading or topic.
3. Prepare duplicated exercise similar to that shown in the example below.

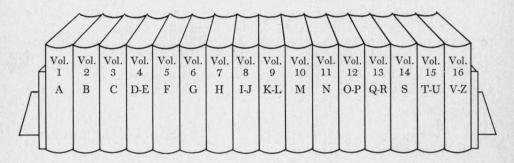

Example: Using the above drawing, in which volume(s) would you likely find the most information about:

1. Soft coal production in Illinois: _____.
2. The Grand Canyon National Park: _____.
3. The population and area of Labrador: _____.
4. Birthplace of Andrew Jackson: _____.
5. Poisonous snakes found in United States: _____.
6. Occupation and nationality of Jan Sibelius: _____.
7. Burial place of U.S. Grant: _____.
8. Site of Olympic Games in 1904 and 1924: _____.
9. Known sources of helium: _____.
10. City in which University of Idaho is located: _____.

"Private Eye" Gets the Facts!

PROCEDURE:

1. Prepare statement sheets with certain facts left blank. The private eye searches through an encyclopedia to find the answers.
2. Cross referencing can be included by asking for a side point on a main reference.
3. The private eye writes the answers.
4. This exercise can be used with a large or small group.

Private Eye exercise about George Washington

1. George Washington was born in the year _____.
2. His mother's name was _____.
3. In his early life Washington was a _____ and surveyed much land.
4. During the French and Indian War he served with General _____.
5. At the time of the American Revolution, Washington was asked to be the _____ of the colonial army.
6. After the war he was asked to be _____ of his country.
7. He died in _____.

Cross References:

1. His mother lived many years in _____, Virginia, where she is buried.
2. General Braddock was from _____.
3. The architect who designed the city of Washington, D.C., was _____.

Private Eye exercise about Martin Luther King, Jr.

1. Martin Luther King was the father of the _____ civil rights movement in the United States.
2. He won the _____ peace prize in _____.
3. King lived in _____, Georgia.
4. His first civil rights demonstration took place in _____, Alabama.
5. King was assassinated _____ in Memphis, Tennessee.
6. King was president of the S_____ C_____ L_____ C_____.
7. King's nonviolent march on Washington, D.C. occurred _____.
8. King is remembered for his work with voter _____ and civil rights _____.

One-a-Day

PROCEDURE:

1. Prepare a number of 3 X 5 cards each of which contains a question which is to be answered using the encyclopedia.
2. Each child has a lined sheet of paper which is labeled "One-a-Day Sheet."
3. Children read as many of the question cards as they wish and select one they wish to answer. The child copies the question and his answer on his One-a-Day Sheet.

VARIATIONS:

1. Children can occasionally exchange their One-a-Day Sheet as a further reading exercise.
2. Once a week, or every two weeks, have pupils select a card and write a story about the topic involved in the question.

Sample Questions:

What is a mongoose?
Is it helpful to people?

Where are the most productive diamond mines?
Can you determine who owns them?

What is The Baseball Hall of Fame?
Where is it located?

Who was the second man to walk on the moon?

Identify Susan B. Anthony.

Who invented the game of basketball?
In what year was the game invented?
Where was basketball first played?

Compare the size of Alaska with that of the continental U.S.

How long have people known about the circulation of blood?

What poisonous snakes are found in the U.S.?

Which are the three largest dams in the U.S.?

Using Maps

Can You Locate the Various States and Major Cities on a Map of the U.S.?

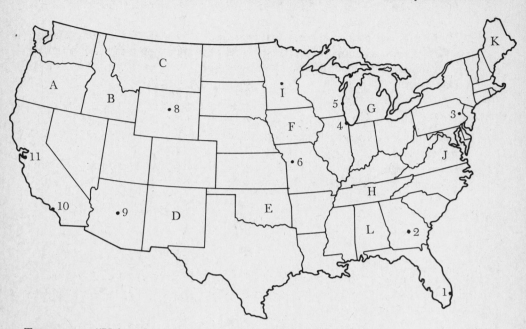

TEACHER: "Using the map above, answer these questions:"

1. What western state is identified by the letter **A**? _____
2. What Atlantic seaboard state is represented by the letter **J**? _____
3. What is the name of the southern state marked **L**? _____
4. Name the southwestern state marked **D**. _____
5. The state marked **G** is the state of _____.
6. The letter **K** is in the state of _____.
7. Two thousand miles to the west, **C** is the state of _____.
8. The number **2** represents the large industrial city of _____ located in the state of _____.
9. The midwestern city (number **4**) is _____.
10. The number **8** represents "the mile high city" of _____.
11. The large eastern city (number **3**) contains many historical sites of the colonial and Revolutionary War periods. It is _____.
12. On the West Coast, number **10** is the city of _____ and number **11** is _____.
13. In the southeast, number **1** is the city of _____.

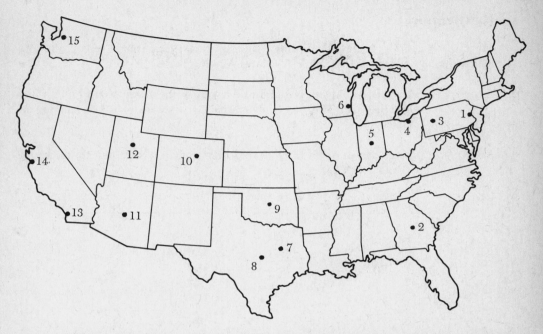

TEACHER: "Use the above map to answer all problems below. In some cases you are to write on the map, in others fill in the blank spaces in the sentence. All numbers on the map represent large or important cities."

1. Write **Iowa** in the proper space on the map.
2. Number **2** on the map represents the location of the city of _____, Georgia.
3. Write **N.D.** and **S.D.** in the states of North Dakota and South Dakota.
4. Write in the abbreviations of three states which border on the Mississippi River. _____, _____, _____
5. The state directly south of the state containing the number **5**, is the state of _____.
6. The state having the longest common border with California is the state of _____. (Write it on the map.)
7. Oklahoma City is number _____.
8. Number **13** on the west coast locates the city of _____.
9. Indianapolis is number _____.
10. Pittsburgh is number _____; Philadelphia is number _____.
11. Cleveland is represented by the number _____.
12. The number _____ represents the city of Milwaukee.
13. Salt Lake City is represented by the number _____ and is located in the state of _____.

Map Reading

Maps often contain guides for finding places or cities. Example A tells us how to locate the city of Detroit. Example B locates Austin, Texas.

Example A: Detroit, Michigan, is found by drawing a line down from **17** and a line over from **F**. The place where the two lines meet is the location of Detroit.

Example B: Lines drawn down from **10** and over from **L** locate the capital city of Texas which is _____.

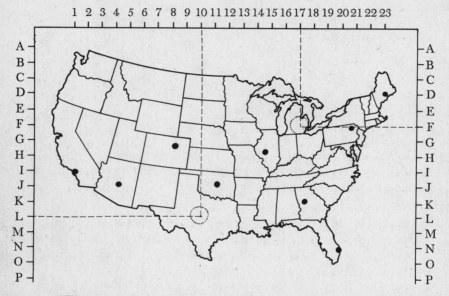

TEACHER: "The problems below provide clues which will guide you to the location of certain cities. You are to name these cities. Complete all the problems you can without using a map. Then use a map of the U.S. if needed. (You need not draw lines on the map; use imaginary lines.)"

1. H—15   Capital of midwestern state; Lincoln buried there. _____
2. D—23   Capital of state located in northeast corner of U.S. _____
3. K—17   Capital and largest industrial city of this southeastern state. _____
4. C—7   Straight lines drawn from these points would intersect in the state of _____.
5. J—4   Capital of southwestern state. _____
6. N—20   Atlantic coastal city. _____
7. G—8   State capital or the "mile high city." _____

Developing Flexible Reading Habits

Rate

PURPOSE: To provide intermediate level students with insights into their reading habits; specifically to provide practice in phrasing in order to increase both rate of reading and comprehension of material.

PROCEDURE: Discuss the fact that as students move upward through the grades they will be expected to do more and more reading. Therefore, they must develop more efficient reading skills. Write the following guidelines on the chalkboard and discuss.

Good readers

> combine words into phrases, and
> read different materials at different rates.

Word-by-Word Reading: A Bad Habit

Word-by-word reading is not efficient and causes one to be a very slow reader. It may also hinder the reader from understanding the meaning of a passage. Each word and its relationship to other words must be kept in mind until the entire sentence is finished. For example, concentrate on each word separately in the following sentence:

The / good / reader / notes / very / quickly / the / difficulty / level / of / the / material / that / he / is / reading. /   If / it / is / easy / he / will / read / faster, / since / he / has / developed / the / ability / to / read / at / different / rates.

Assume that a child reads all the time the way you read this sentence. The teacher should suggest that the student read the passage again saying, "Read it like you would say it," or "Read it with expression." When people read with expression they group words into logical thought units and read phrases as single units.

Read the same sentence again. It is arranged in phrases.

The good reader   notes very quickly   the difficulty level of the material   that he is reading.   If it is easy he will read faster   since he has developed   the ability to read at different rates.

Test on Phrase Reading

PROCEDURE: The material below consists of phrases which gradually increase in length. Read down the columns. Try to read each phrase as one unit. Can you read the longer phrases as one unit?

can be	go now	try one
is a job	to a man	gave help
see it now	be so kind	one for all
fire at will	just so long	hear the bell
generally fair	will come soon	is well to take
change the parts	around the earth	became the rivals
difficult to trace	during this period	measured accurately
men worked for years	accurate observation	heard a lively debate

Practice Material: Medium length, unrelated phrases.

Read down each column as rapidly as you can. Treat each line or phrase as one thought unit.

pet the dog	went to see	for instance
that is all	a way out	is very busy
saves times	adding to it	out of step
want to go	to the lake	clean it up
pointed out	not too easy	in the attic
lay it down	a big help	two or three
to the lake	did not go	at the farm
on the paper	read a story	to the house
eat some cake	on the slide	did not fall
in the shade	the big horse	word groups
at one time	in spite of	try to meet
set the stage	can be done	so will we
get the facts	some do not	it was sold
was not easy	is also used	best of luck
a question of	likely to fail	into the park

Phrase Reading: Continued Text

PROCEDURE: Read down the columns as rapidly as you can. Read them several times and try to improve your rate.

Many students
feel that they
do not read
as effectively
as they should.
These students
are probably
correct.
    You can be
a better reader
by improving
your present
reading habits.
One important
reading skill
is *phrasing*.
Phrasing means
saying words
in groups.
In learning
to read
you probably
read each word
separately.
This is called
word-by-word
reading.

You should not
be reading
this way now.
When one reads
word-by-word
he or she reads slowly.
In addition
the meaning
of sentences
and paragraphs
is often lost
because words
are not combined
into logical
thought units.
    This material
is arranged
in phrases.
Each line
should be read
as one unit.
These lines
of print
are no longer
than some
single words.
You can read

longer words
as one unit.
For instance,
    Mississippi
    thunderstorm
    comprehension
    association
    combination.
    With practice
you can also
learn to read
several words
just as easily
as you read
longer words.
You simply
combine words
into single
thought units.
    This material
is provided
for practice
in reading phrases.
When you read
other material
you can do
your own phrasing.

Your Phrasing Pattern

PROCEDURE: In the following sentence the spaces represent one way that the material could be phrased.

> *Today   one will find   very few positions   of responsibility   in   business   or industry   which   do not call for   extensive reading.*

You can discover the pattern of phrasing that you use when reading. The material in the box below is taken from *The Declaration of Independence*. Read it through once. Then underline the words and groups of words which you read as units. Doing this task may provide insight for answering the following questions.

1. Do you tend to read word-by-word?
2. If you read in phrases, do you vary the length of the phrase? do you read in logical thought units?

We hold these truths to be self-evident, that all men are created equal, that they are endowed by their Creator with certain unalienable Rights, that among these are Life, Liberty and the pursuit of Happiness. That to secure these rights, Governments are instituted among Men, deriving their just powers from the consent of the governed. That whenever any Form of Government becomes destructive of these ends, it is the Right of the People to alter or to abolish it, and to institute new Government, laying its foundation on such principles and organizing its powers in such form, as to them shall seem most likely to affect their Safety and Happiness.

(See page 128 to compare your phrasing with another model.)

More About Reading

This exercise
also provides
some material
which is phrased
in small units.
As you read,
your eyes move
fairly rapidly
down the page.
This is similar
to reading
a newspaper.

This material
is written
in short phrases
so that you
can practice
seeing words
in thought units.
This helps you
read faster.
However,
remember also
that reading
in phrases
or thought units
helps the reader
get the meaning.

When one reads
word-by-word
he or she must select
groups of words
that make sense.

Good readers
have developed
the ability
to read
some materials
more rapidly
than others.
More important
they also know
when they should
slow down.

There are many
reading skills
that combine
to produce
efficient readers.
These skills
also influence
how rapidly
one can read.
For example,
good readers
have a large

sight vocabulary.
(Words which one
does not need
to study
or "sound out.")
Efficient readers
know the meanings
of many words,
as well as
different meanings
for the same word.
They read widely,
which develops
background.
This helps them
understand
more of what
they read.
Good readers
profit from
punctuation marks,
they read with
good expression.
But above all
they like to read.
One might say
"Good readers
are avid readers."

Declaration of Independence

. . . —We hold
these truths
to be self-evident,
that all men
are created equal,
that they are endowed
by their Creator
with certain
unalienable Rights,
that among these
are Life,
Liberty
and the pursuit
of Happiness.
That to secure
these rights,
Governments
are instituted
among Men,
deriving
their just powers
from the consent
of the governed,
That whenever
any Form
of Government
becomes destructive
of these ends,
it is the Right
of the People
to alter
or to abolish it,
and to institute
new Government,
laying its foundation

on such principles
and organizing
its powers
in such form,
as to them
shall seem
most likely
to effect
their Safety
and Happiness.
Prudence, indeed,
will dictate
that Governments
long established
should not
be changed
for light
and transient causes;
and accordingly
all experience
hath shewn
that mankind
are more disposed
to suffer,
while evils are sufferable,
than to right themselves
by abolishing
the forms to which
they are accustomed.
But when
a long train
of abuses
and usurpations, . . .
evinces a design
to reduce them
under absolute

Despotism,
it is their right,
it is their duty,
to throw off
such Government,
and to provide
new Guards
for their future
security. . . .
    WE, THEREFORE,
the Representatives
of the UNITED STATES
OF AMERICA,
in General Congress,
Assembled, . . .
do, in the Name,
and by Authority
of the good People
of these Colonies,
solemnly publish
and declare,
That these
United Colonies are,
and of Right ought
to be FREE AND
INDEPENDENT STATES, . . .
And for the support
of this Declaration,
with a firm reliance
on the protection
of divine Providence,
we mutually pledge
to each other
our Lives,
our Fortunes
and our sacred Honor.

Teachers' Declaration of Independence

In conclusion,
we, teachers of reading,
who, having noted
that many children
do not perceive
learning to read
as a joyful
happy experience,
and furthermore
on occasion
having noted
that teaching reading
is not as rewarding
as we know
it should be,
we do now
solemnly swear,
(or where swearing
is frowned upon
or prohibited by law),
do solemnly affirm
that henceforth
we will improve
classroom vibrations
by helping children
to see that reading
is a language process.
Schools are instituted
in all societies
without the consent
of children.
Nor are the learners
inquired of,
relative to
the curriculum
or the methodology
through which it passes.

We hold
that when instruction
becomes destructive to
the joy of learning
that instruction
should be abolished
or modified
in such manner
as to lead
potential learners
to experience
the power,
the beauty,
and the magic
of their language.
We pledge allegiance
to the space program,
to past and future
explorations.
And yes, Virginia,
children should have
the right to read.
A catchy slogan,
unless they also have
the will to read
and the need to read.

With a firm reliance
on the magic of language
and in the name
of children everywhere,
and by authority
granted us by sundry
teaching certificates,
we mutually pledge
to smuggle language
into reading instruction.